Praise for

"This is an interesting text written in a conversational tone by an author who is knowledgeable about technology and enthusiastic about the potential of flipping as a technique to alter teaching and learning. Well-written case studies from various classrooms provide insight into what flipping means as a part of instruction."

Dr. Allen D. Glenn, Retired Professor and Dean Emeritus
College of Education, University of Washington
Seattle, WA

"This great book provides the background, reasons, and advantages of flipping. It is the perfect book for someone trying to decide whether or not to get their feet wet. It also offers resources for further in-depth study and collaboration."

Alexis Ludewig, Supervisor of Student Teachers
University of Wisconsin Oshkosh
Oshkosh, WI

"This book addresses some of the basic inadequacies in our traditional educational practice. It provides an innovative and thoughtful alternative to the all too prevalent non-student-centered approach that has dominated education for too long."

Robert Barkley, Jr., Retired Executive Director
Ohio Education Association
Worthington, OH

"I highly recommend this book for any educator interested in flipping the classroom to reinvent the learning process. The stories show how flipping is energizing teachers and students—with powerful results!"

Lisa Schmucki
Founder and CEO of edweb.net

"Flipped classrooms empower teachers to engage students in deeper learning. This book gives readers 10 reasons for joining forces to make this possibility a reality."

Tom Carroll, President
National Commission on
Teaching and America's Future (NCTAF)

For Harry
Who still makes my heart flip

And for Joseph and Dominick, Jeffrey and Magnolia
Our beautiful future

Time for Learning

Top 10 Reasons Why Flipping the Classroom Can Change Education

Kathleen P. Fulton

CORWIN
A SAGE Company

CORWIN
A SAGE Company

FOR INFORMATION:

Corwin
A SAGE Company
2455 Teller Road
Thousand Oaks, California 91320
(800) 233-9936
www.corwin.com

SAGE Publications Ltd.
1 Oliver's Yard
55 City Road
London EC1Y 1SP
United Kingdom

SAGE Publications India Pvt. Ltd.
B 1/I 1 Mohan Cooperative Industrial Area
Mathura Road, New Delhi 110 044
India

SAGE Publications Asia-Pacific Pte. Ltd.
3 Church Street
#10-04 Samsung Hub
Singapore 049483

Printed in the United States of America

Library of Congress Cataloging-in-Publication Data

Fulton, Kathleen.

Time for learning : top 10 reasons why flipping the classroom can change education / Kathleen P. Fulton.

pages cm
Includes bibliographical references and index.

ISBN 978-1-4833-3281-9 (pbk.)

1. Blended learning. 2. Homework—Computer network resources. I. Title.

LB1028.5F857 2014
371.3—dc23   2014001787

This book is printed on acid-free paper.

Executive Editor: Arnis Burvikovs
Associate Editor: Desirée A. Bartlett
Editorial Assistant: Ariel Price
Production Editor: Melanie Birdsall
Copy Editor: Cate Huisman
Typesetter: C&M Digitals (P) Ltd.
Proofreader: Annie Lubinsky
Indexer: Molly Hall
Cover Designer: Rose Storey
Marketing Manager: MaryEllin Santiago

SUSTAINABLE FORESTRY INITIATIVE
Certified Chain of Custody
Promoting Sustainable Forestry
www.sfiprogram.org
SFI-01268
SFI label applies to text stock

14 15 16 17 18 10 9 8 7 6 5 4 3 2 1

Contents

Preface

WHY A BOOK ON FLIPPED CLASSROOMS?

Over the past 25 years, I've written a lot about educational technologies and school change, but I never heard the term "flipping the classroom" until I attended the Intel Schools of Distinction awards dinner in the fall of 2011. I was seated at a table with a group of amazing educators from Byron Independent School District #531 in northeastern Minnesota. Their high school was nominated for an Intel award based on the changes they had made to their math curriculum. The teachers enthusiastically shared with me the story of how, when there was no money to buy new textbooks, they decided to create their own curriculum, delivering math lessons using an interactive whiteboard and posting them on YouTube for students to watch at night, then using their class time to work with students as they tackled the math problems raised in the lessons they had viewed the night before.

This, I learned, was called "flipping the classroom." I was captivated by their story and totally charmed by their passion for what they were doing. When the announcement was made that Byron won the high school mathematics award for 2011 Intel School of Distinction, I leapt to my feet and cheered alongside them!

Following the awards ceremony, I suggested to Wendy Shannon, then superintendent of the district, that I'd be honored to write an article about the Byron story. She loved the idea! Thus began my explorations into the world of flipped classrooms. Since that time I have visited, interviewed, and explored the work of teachers who were flipping in a variety of settings: urban and rural, public and private, elementary, middle, and high school. What strikes me about all of these educators is their creativity, enthusiasm, and willingness to share what they are learning with others. I saw how flipped teaching opens the door of the classroom and lets teachers showcase what they do, explore what is working and question what is not, and learn from one another. These teachers are my inspiration; it was they who motivated me to write this book.

HOW THIS BOOK IS DIFFERENT

This book is not intended as a sales pitch for flipping or the products teachers use to support the practice. It offers a balanced picture of flipping from a variety of perspectives—those of teachers, administrators, and researchers as well as students and their parents. Although my tone is generally positive, I end each chapter with a series of caveats to provide reminders of the potential downsides and unintended consequences, positive and negative, that can accompany educational and technological innovations.

Nor is this book intended to serve as a "how to" book. There are a number of other excellent books, videos, blogs, websites, and other resources that give detailed guidance in the technical details of flipping classrooms. These are best written by teachers themselves, drawing on their classroom experience and knowledge of emerging technologies and capabilities. I reference some of these in the book chapters, as well as in the Q & A in the appendix.

Finally, this book is not a series of case studies selected to show "the best of flipping." Rather, I use teachers' stories and words as snapshots, selected to illustrate key points and various ways teachers are flipping across the curriculum and at various grade levels.

My goal in *Time for Learning: Top 10 Reasons Why Flipping the Classroom Can Change Education* is to explore ideas and analyses beyond what current publications have to offer. I portray flipping in the context of school change over time, especially changes driven by technology. I also explore the implications for powerful new approaches to teaching based on research on cognition, pedagogy, and learning theory. This book also offers a nuanced view and analysis of potential impacts on teachers (their roles, deployment, and work in teams rather than as sole artisans), and about implications for policy. The focus is on K–12 schools and schooling, but examples from higher education are included where they offer useful insights.

WHO CAN BENEFIT FROM THIS BOOK?

This book is aimed at several audiences. For those teachers already flipping the classroom, I hope this book resonates with what you are doing and why. In the midst of a revolution, it can be useful to step back and see how what you are doing fits into the larger picture. I know you are always eager to get your hands on any and all information about the field, one in which you take great interest and justifiable pride as early adopters. You will be the ones to let me know if I got the story right, and I welcome your comments!

Beyond these trailblazing advocates, however, my primary audience is traditional educators at all levels who have heard the buzz about flipped classrooms and are curious to learn more. Whether you are a classroom teacher, resource teacher, teacher candidate or teacher educator, or a principal or school administrator, this book will provide the overview you need to know about flipped teaching and considerations to keep in mind if you plan to adopt it for your school or classroom.

- Teachers will read it from the perspective of improving practice and engaging students.
- Principals will find value in the discussion of remodeling education and using educational resources differently.

- **Superintendents** will find this an important reference as they provide leadership that promotes school change, or are asked to support innovation driven from the bottom up by their teachers.

In addition, education policy makers at all levels can gain from reading this book:

- **School board members** seeking to keep abreast of educational innovations
- **Legislators and staffers at the state or national level** considering the implications of flipped classrooms and the policies that can support or (impede) their effectiveness

Others I hope find value in the book include the following:

- **Researchers** investigating the impacts of flipping and approaches most conducive to success
- **International educators** seeking to learn from innovative practices in U.S. schools
- And, importantly, **parents, the media, and members of the general public** who wish to stay informed of important trends impacting today's students

I hope this book encourages all readers to consider new possibilities—to flip your mindset—as together we reimagine and refine ways to harness our most powerful assets—great teachers, curious students, and powerful tools—to expand the time for learning for all students.

Acknowledgments

This book would not have been possible without the inspiration and guidance of many, many teachers who graciously shared their time, stories, and enthusiasm for flipped classrooms. Not every story made it into this book, but all of your stories were guideposts for me along the way. For those whose classrooms I was able to spotlight, I hope I gave justice to the excitement and creativity of what you do, every day, to inspire your students to take charge of their learning and seek knowledge and beauty in all they do.

Special thanks go to those who introduced me to flipped classrooms: the amazing educators at Byron High School. Former superintendent Wendy Shannon was the first to encourage me to write about flipping; she started me on this new adventure. Math department chair Troy Faulkner has been my go-to teacher, answering my e-mail questions almost before I could push "send"! Troy was especially helpful in assisting with the Q & A at the end of this book. Rob Warnecke, the Jens—Jennifer Green and Jennifer Hegna, principal Mike Duffy, superintendent Jeff Elstad, and all the educators at Byron are indeed terrific!

I also want to thank my friends in higher education and industry, who gave me thoughtful assistance in key areas. John Bransford's unbounded enthusiasm—showering me with papers and ideas—helped me wade through the thickets of cognitive science research. Eric Mazur was equally responsive to my questions regarding peer learning. The educators cited in Chapter 10 thoughtfully responded to my questionnaire, adding wise perspectives that helped frame my thinking about the future of flipping. Bror Saxberg was particularly helpful in offering suggestions related to learning theory. My longtime critical friend Allen Glenn kept me honest and grounded, as always! The team at Corwin: Desirée Bartlett, Melanie Birdsall, Cate Huisman, Ariel Price, and Rose Storey were terrific to work with—responsive, professional, and helpful at every stage. Special thanks go to my wise and wonderful Corwin executive editor Arnis Burvikovs, who invited me to write this book, and kept me moving forward with his unflagging encouragement and enthusiasm for the project.

Loving personal friends held my hand through the process of getting this, my first book, off the ground. Steve Tullberg, bless his heart, read the first draft and gave me great suggestions. The gang at Chill Week freed me from kitchen duties so I could write while on vacation at the Doubs' Bluff Pointe paradise. My techie-pal Susan Jones, channeling our dear Nancy Martin, encouraged me to make this book happen!

Of course, my wonderful husband, Harry, was there all along, patient and enthusiastic, nudging me along this great adventure. You, Jeff and Magdalena, Rebecca and Jim, and our four grandchildren are my life's joy.

PUBLISHER'S ACKNOWLEDGMENTS

Corwin gratefully acknowledges the contributions of the following reviewers:

Robert (Bob) Barkley Jr.
Retired Executive Director
Ohio Education Association

David Callaway
Seventh-Grade Social Studies Teacher
Rocky Heights Middle School
Highlands Ranch, CO

Tom Carroll
President
National Commission on Teaching
   and America's Future (NCTAF)

Dr. Allen D. Glenn
Retired Professor and Dean Emeritus
College of Education, University of Washington
Seattle, WA

Alexis Ludewig
Supervisor of Student Teachers
University of Wisconsin Oshkosh
Oshkosh, WI

Lisa Schmucki
Founder and CEO of edweb.net

Dr. Gary L. Willhite
Professor
University of Wisconsin La Crosse
La Crosse, WI

About the Author

Photo by Harry J. Fulton

Kathleen P. Fulton is a writer and education consultant specializing in teaching quality and technology. She served as director, Reinventing Schools for the 21st Century, at the National Commission on Teaching and America's Future (NCTAF) for 10 years. Before joining NCTAF, Ms. Fulton was project director for the Congressional Web-Based Education Commission and lead author of their report, *The Power of the Internet for Learning*. She spent four years as Associate Director of the Center for Learning and Educational Technology at the University of Maryland, and worked for ten years as a policy analyst for the Congressional Office of Technology Assessment (OTA). At OTA she was the project director responsible for several major education reports, including *Education and Technology: Future Visions*, and *Teachers and Technology: Making the Connection*.

Since her retirement from NCTAF, Fulton has been consulting with a range of clients, including the State Education Technology Directors Association, the U.S. Department of State, the University of Colorado at Denver, the National Council of Teachers of English, and the Byron School District in Minnesota. Her current work focuses on flipped classrooms, and she has written articles on this topic for *Phi Delta Kappan*, *T.H.E. Journal*, *Learning and Leading with Technology*, and *School Administrator*. She graduated from Smith College with a BA in English and received an MA in Human Development from the University of Maryland. Fulton lives in Takoma Park, Maryland, with her husband, Harry Fulton, and has two grown children, Rebecca and Jeffrey, and four amazing grandchildren.

Introduction

High School Math

Troy Faulkner, Byron High School, Byron, Minnesota

Troy Faulkner teaches today very differently than he did before. "I used to be the one doing all the work," he recalls.

> I lectured and worked on the math problems, while the students sat passively listening, or not listening, as was sometimes the case! Now they can no longer sit back and watch me do the math. They have to be the active ones—it's their job to solve the math problems. But I'm constantly moving about the class, working with them one-on-one or in small groups: watching and listening; questioning and suggesting; encouraging and nudging; demonstrating and jumping on those just-in-time, just-what's-needed teachable moments when a student really is ready to learn.

Here's what his class looks like today: At some point before class begins (the night before, or in the morning before school begins, or during lunch), his students watch a 10- to 15-minute video lesson taught by Faulkner or another Byron math teacher who covers the same course in other sections. As soon as students enter his class, they start on the first of several "peer instruction" problems written on the white board that require them to apply concepts from the video lesson. After answering the question on their own, they discuss their answers and procedures with the students near them. If they disagree on a problem, each must try to convince the others why her or his method and answer is correct. They must come to an agreement on the correct answer or solution and frame their reasons why they support this solution. According to Faulkner,

> the students are emotionally involved in their learning, because they must defend their answers. Plus they are really curious: "Is my answer the right one?" It's a deeper level of understanding as they work through their reasoning and put that reasoning into words.

He listens to the group responses and determines whether there's been enough disagreement or confusion to warrant reviewing the concept with the class as a whole. After three or four rounds of this cycle of problem solving, sharing, and debating the peer instruction questions, students spend the remainder of the class working through the rest of their math problems around the assigned topic, helping each other as needed. Faulkner walks around the room, helping small groups working together. He's alert to the students who seem to be struggling but haven't asked questions, and he often sits with them to help them or pairs them up with others who are comfortable with the particular topic. He calls it "controlled chaos," but that's okay with him if everyone is engaged and learning.

Source: T. Faulkner (personal communication, September 20, 2013, and October 3, 2011)

This example illustrates how one teacher has changed his classroom, his teaching, and his students' mode of learning by flipping the classroom. But haven't cutting-edge teachers always been trying new things, willing to take risks (at the "bleeding edge" of change) to improve their students' chances of success? How different is flipping, and what can innovators like Faulkner tell us about where education may be headed?

America's education system has been compared to a battleship: big and ponderous, slow to change direction. Buzzing around this mighty enterprise are a flotilla of fads: innovations in content, teaching tools, pedagogical styles, theories, resources, and school designs. They pop up, gain attention, and typically fade from view as yet another educational innovation takes the place of the newest new thing. Teachers complain of reform du jour, and the public is confused, yearning for the good old days of the schools they knew, schools that they believe worked just fine for them!

Flipped classrooms could be the latest hot topic in K–12 education. The concept has recently captured the interest of educators all over the United States and beyond. There is an organization of teachers interested in flipping, and there are online communities, blogs, and NINGs along with websites, videos, books, and articles. Two pioneering educators who popularized the idea—Aaron Sams and Jonathan Bergmann— have become virtual rock stars of flipping.

Beyond the hype, there is solid work being done by creative and deeply committed educators around the country, and there are many good reasons for the interest in flipping. But before we look at the top 10 reasons why flipped classrooms could change education, some background will be useful.

WHAT IS FLIPPING ANYWAY?

Webster's first definition of the verb flip is "to toss" ("Flip," 1939); Macmillan's online dictionary defines it as "to turn over quickly, or to make something turn over" ("Flip," n.d.). These definitions make the flipping-the-classroom metaphor interesting: Are we tossing out the old, or turning over our way of teaching from what was done before?

The term *flip the classroom* refers to inverting the traditional method of teaching; that is, turning upside down the model in which information (the teaching lesson) is presented during class time, and homework is assigned for practice at home. As the above case demonstrates, in flipped teaching (or flipped learning, as some prefer), the teaching lesson is assigned for students to access out of class time, freeing up class time for building on that lesson with discussion, exercises, labs, or projects. It is just that simple, and just that revolutionary.

HOW DO TEACHERS CREATE FLIPPED LESSONS?

There is no one recipe or template for flipped lessons. Typically, lessons are captured in video format, prepared or curated by teachers. Most flipping teachers produce their own lessons and can be "present" in the video in a variety of ways: They can teach the lesson and be shown full-on teaching, or narrate the lesson while appearing in a small corner of a slide, or provide the voice in the background describing the action on a whiteboard or computer screen. Some flipped lessons aren't the teacher's own delivery of content at all; rather, the teacher may assign lessons recorded by other teachers or use videos from educational or entertainment sources online that highlight the teaching concept (e.g., a video of three different versions of a scene in a Shakespearean play). The content—problems from a textbook, demonstrations of an experiment, readings from an original source, illustrations from website or other resource—is as variable as is, well, content.

There is a growing base of software and applications for capturing this content—on audio files, video files, PowerPoint presentations, or screenshot captures of a teacher working on a whiteboard. Whatever the format, the student accesses the information portion of the lesson at home or out of class and then works on it when in the classroom with the teacher and other students.

HOW DIFFERENT IS FLIPPING?

Teachers have always expected students to absorb content as part of their homework. In English classes, teachers assign novels, plays, or poems to be read at home so that class time can be spent discussing the content. History teachers assign chapters in history texts as a basis for classroom work. Nevertheless, for most teachers in most subjects most of the time, class time is when the majority of content is presented and lessons are delivered.

What is different in flipping is that the actual lesson on which the text, problem, or chapter is based—the teacher-added content—is the work assigned for out of class, offloaded and sent home for students to review on their own time. Students are expected to access and absorb the content *before* class, not through lectures they listen to during the class period. In contrast to the traditional teaching model, in which students come to class to get information, in a flipped model students come to class prepared to discuss, analyze, practice, or apply the information they accessed and absorbed before class.

Without the interruptions of class disruptions, teacher-delivered content can be distilled into short modules, ideally no more than 10–15 minutes each (even shorter for younger children). The student can replay and review each lesson as many times as needed. When students enter the classroom, the teacher assigns activities to practice, deepen, and assess understanding.

Technology gives teachers the opportunity to provide lesson content in a variety of formats and enables students to control both the time when and the speed at which they get the information—and to rewind and review the lessons as often as necessary.

· THE FLIPPING MINDSET

Educators like Cheryl Morris suggest that flipping shouldn't be seen as a pedagogy, or instructional technique, or even a theory. Instead, she describes what she calls the "flipping mindset," which involves three elements:

1. Teachers make the best use of their face-to-face time with students.

2. The classroom uses student-centered pedagogy.

3. There is an intentional focus on higher-level thinking, rather than rote memorization. (Morris, Thomasson, Lindgren-Streicher, Kirch, & Baker, 2012)

A more expanded version of this was defined by the Flipped Learning Network in their 2013 study "A Review of Flipped Learning" (Hamdan, McKnight, McKnight, & Arfstrom, 2013). Using the acronym FLIP as an organizing framework, they identified (and even trademarked!) what they call essential elements, unifying themes or requirements for what they call the "Four pillars of F-L-I-P":

Flexible environments (in terms of timelines, student groupings, assessments, and learning spaces),

Learning culture (a culture built around the learners' needs, as opposed to a teacher-centered classroom),

Intentional content (teachers designing instruction in a variety of formats to assure contextual understanding and procedural fluency), and

Professional educators (good teachers are critically important though perhaps less visibly present).

A BRIEF HISTORY OF FLIPPING

Technology has always been a magnet for those who want to do things faster, better, and, ideally, cheaper. For educators, this means finding better ways to reach students effectively and help them learn.

Lessons From Higher Education

Research coming out of higher education provided guideposts and inspiration for creative educators at the K–12 level. The work of Harvard physics professor Eric Mazur has been cited by many as a source of inspiration because of his interest in how technology makes it possible to engage students more actively in their own learning. As early as 1991, Mazur described how he created tutorial text, in the form of electronic note cards that distilled—from thousand-page physics tomes—the essence of key topics studied in an introductory physics course (Mazur, 1991). Mazur was encouraged by the way these resources allowed the students to engage with the content as needed (e.g., clicking on words for definitions or what he called "zoom icons" for a fuller discussion of a topic). He explored how the students could use these outside of class to go deeper into the content of traditional lectures. Mazur's continuing research and practice around teaching for greater student engagement and learning—with or without technology—and his explorations into ways of blending content delivery out of class with student cooperative learning and discussion within class, led to his leadership in the field of peer instruction, a topic we describe more in Chapter 3.

Other educators in colleges and universities were also looking at how the content delivered to students in large lecture halls could be provided more efficiently and effectively. Few lecturers can keep every student in a lecture hall spellbound for the entire class period; most are lucky if they keep the majority of them awake until the end of class! But with advances in technology, it became obvious that the basic information delivery system—the lecture—could be videorecorded. Students could watch the lectures on their own devices, on their own time.

In 2000, educators at Miami University published a paper describing what they called "inverted instruction" or "inverted classrooms" for teaching economics (Lage, Platt, & Treglia, 2000). The inverted classroom was one in which "events that have traditionally taken place inside the classroom now take place outside the classroom and vice versa" (p. 32). For them, inverting instruction meant using the technologies of the day—the World Wide Web, multimedia computers, and VCRs—to deliver lectures that students watched in computer labs or at home. Students then did their homework in groups in class. Although they did not call this flipping, it was an early precursor of today's model in K–12 education

Blended Learning and Online Content for K–12

Online courses were also catching on at the K–12 level, and blended learning became a term for mixing online courses with teacher-directed support in the classroom. Even teachers who were not involved with online courses were discovering the rich treasure trove of free lectures on videos they could download from the Internet. The largest and best known of these free lesson resources is Khan Academy.

Salman Khan began making videos and posting them on YouTube in 2004. His goal was a simple one: He wanted to help his seventh-grade cousin Nadia, who was struggling with algebra. But Khan was in Boston and Nadia was in New Orleans. Unable to tutor her by sitting down next to her, he recorded himself working the problems, discussing what he was doing and why, in short videos he uploaded onto YouTube for her to review. The video tutorials helped Nadia and, to Khan's amazed delight, other learners and teachers began using his video lessons.

Khan began making video lessons covering a range of topics and levels, from basic arithmetic to advanced calculus, from economics and history to astronomy. In 2010 Bill Gates, who had been following Khan's videos and using them to teach his own children, promoted Khan's videos at a conference and others quickly signed on. Gates invested $15 million in Khan Academy to meet the goal of offering free, high-quality education to anyone with access to the Internet. The Gates grant and support from Google and others made it possible for Khan to hire engineers and designers to pilot new software, including a sophisticated dashboard for tracking student progress.

Today Khan Academy offers thousands of video lessons, along with assessment tools for "coaches," who may be teachers, parents, employers, or friends, located throughout the world. And it's all free (Khan Academy, n.d.).

Bergmann and Sams: Flipping's Early Rock Stars

Teachers in K–12 schools were also beginning to experiment with ways of teaching that used video lessons from a range of sources. While it is likely that some educators were already putting their lessons online for students to watch outside of class, Jonathan Bergmann and Aaron Sams are credited with being the ones to popularize the idea of flipped classrooms in the K–12 sector.

In 2006, Bergmann and Sams were high school chemistry teachers in Woodland Park, Colorado, a mountain community west of Colorado Springs. They were concerned about the amount of class time their students were missing when the students travelled long distances to participate in sports and other activities. Every time a student missed a class, the student was in danger of falling behind. Being conscientious teachers, Sams and Bergman spent what they called "inordinate amounts of time reteaching lessons to students who missed class" (Bergman & Sams, 2012, p. 3). There had to be a better way.

The light bulb went on when Sams learned about a way to put slides, voice, and audio onto a video file that could be placed online. They tried it and, once they began to provide the videos to students who had missed classes, other students began asking for the opportunity to watch their lectures as well. Students asking permission to watch more teaching—how great is that? The videos generated so much interest among their students that Bergmann and Sams decided they would prerecord all their chemistry classes for the 2007–08 school year.

They participated in online forums with other science teachers and made their videos available online. Soon other teachers began to try the videos with their classes. The idea took off. Sams and Bergmann were featured on the local TV station, other districts invited them to share what they were doing, and a movement had begun. What they first called *reverse instruction* became known as *flipped instruction*, now commonly referred to as the *flipped classroom model, flipped teaching, flipped learning,* or just *flipping*.

HOW COMMON ARE FLIPPED CLASSROOMS?

What began as a teacher-led, bottom-up movement has now become a thriving market as demand increases for examples, training, tools, and services related to flipped teaching. Webinars and videos, books, professional development courses, tools, and products promoting flipping have begun to flood the market. At the same time, teacher-led discussion groups, blogs, and online communities are blossoming as teachers reach out to share their experiences, frustrations, and tips with one another.

The speed at which flipping has spread reflects the power of the Internet as a viral agent for innovation. Educators can see flipping in action with videos posted on YouTube and learn about it through groups like the Flipped Learning Network, whose NING discussion group had 16,000 members as of fall 2013. Their webinars and podcasts regularly attract thousands of participants around the world. Online professional communities like EdWeb's Flipped Learning Community have also grown rapidly.

Nonetheless, this still represents only a small slice of the teaching workforce. A 2013 report from Project Tomorrow, summarizing the results of their 2012 online survey of over 100,000 K–12 educators, provides a window into how many and what types of teachers are flipping their classrooms (Project Tomorrow, 2013b). At the time they conducted their survey, only 9% of their surveyed teachers reported they were flipping, with 6% saying they were using videos they found online and 3% using video lessons or lectures they themselves created. Flipping was most common among science and math teachers, 15% of whom reported they were already flipping their classes. Of the science and math teachers not yet flipping, 23% said they were interested in doing so.

Data from the 2013 survey shed further light on why flipping may take time to take hold. In that survey, 15% of teachers surveyed indicated they were interested in trying flipping, but more (19%) said they had heard about it and were not interested. It appears that a lack of good information about how to make flipping work remains a barrier, as 42% of teachers were concerned their students would not be able to access the videos at home, 19% said they would need instruction in making videos or finding high-quality videos online, and 16% indicated they would need instruction on how to best utilize classroom time in the flipped teaching model (Project Tomorrow and Flipped Learning Network, 2014).

Interest shown by school leaders may soon impact these numbers, as 40% of school site administrators in the 2013 survey indicated that they were encouraging teachers to implement flipping this year. When asked to rate a number of currently popular approaches to digital learning for their impact on transforming teaching and learning within their districts, 17% of school site administrators, and 25% of district administrators, ranked flipping as having the greatest impact (Project Tomorrow and Flipped Learning Network, 2014). Nevertheless, whole school implementation is still rare. Schools like Michigan's Clintondale High School (www.flippedhigh school.com), declared a "totally flipped high school" in 2012 (see Chapter 4), are still the exception rather than the rule among schools where flipped teaching occurs.

WILL FLIPPING EXACERBATE THE DIGITAL DIVIDE?

One of the most common questions posed about flipped classrooms is "What about students who don't have access to the Internet for watching lessons at home? Won't these students be penalized by their lack of access and fall further behind?" It's an important question, reflected in the teacher concerns reported above. Proponents of flipping suggest that there are a number of reasons why this could pose less of a concern than might be expected. As discussed in Chapter 8, school technology resources are expanding across the board, and many of the tools required for producing and distributing flipped lessons are either already in place in schools, or soon

Table 1   Options for Delivery of Flipped Lessons

If a student has. . . .	Then . . .
Computer with Internet capability and service	Lessons can be watched on desktop at home, laptop at home, or outside school.
Computer with no Internet	Lessons can be burned onto a DVD or flash drive and sent home with student.
Tablet or smartphone with Internet access (wireless or 3G/4G)	Lessons can be watched anywhere, anytime when wireless or 3G/4G service is available.
No personal technology, but the school has adequate technology	Laptops or tablets can be loaned to students as needed.
No personal technology, and school technology resources are limited	Students can watch lessons in school computer labs, libraries, or classrooms before or after class.

will be available as part of schools' planning for technology upgrades. Furthermore, recognizing that increasing numbers of students have smartphones and tablets or other mobile devices, many schools are encouraging BYOD (Bring Your Own Device) initiatives to supplement school resources.

Nonetheless, teachers who are considering flipping their classrooms should ensure that all students will have easy access to their lessons before they start. Many teachers survey students and parents about home technology resources and Internet connectivity (see Chapter 7), and then arrange for one or more of the solutions outlined in Table 1.

WHY IS FLIPPING CATCHING FIRE? READ ON!

In this book I suggest 10 reasons that the experts—teachers— suggest are motivations for flipping their classrooms. The number 10 is an arbitrary figure (reminding us of the zany top 10 lists created by David Letterman on his late night talk show!), but it provides a framework for going deeper into arguments for flipped teaching and learning. These reasons are complementary, blending and reinforcing each other. Importantly, each of these reasons comes with its own set of caveats and warnings to bear in mind. These caveats are presented at the end of each chapter, along with a brief summary of the chapter's key points.

- **Chapter 1: Flipping Maximizes Time for Active Learning.** This is the most compelling reason to flip: maximizing the use of valuable time a teacher has to spend face-to-face working with students in the classroom—time that has been freed up from lecturing.

- **Chapter 2: Flipping Facilitates Differentiated Instruction.** Teachers have more time to watch their students at work, help them individually, and differentiate instruction based on individual student needs and successes.

- **Chapter 3: Flipping Is Grounded in Learning Theory.** When done well, flipped teaching uses pedagogical principles that rest on a solid base of learning theory and cognitive research.

- **Chapter 4: Flipping Effectiveness Data Show Promise.** Although the data are limited, this chapter presents what is known to date about outcomes, describing impacts on student achievement, motivation, and engagement.

- **Chapter 5: Flipping Benefits Teachers Too.** The linchpin to success is the teacher; this chapter discusses how flipping impacts teachers in terms of their roles, learning, and professionalism.

- **Chapter 6: Students Like Flipping.** One of the key inspirations for teachers is how much their students prefer flipped classrooms to traditional classrooms.

- **Chapter 7: Flipping Brings the Classroom to Parents.** Things are flipped at home when teachers send video instruction home for students to watch out of class; parents need preparation for these changes.

- **Chapter 8: Flipping Makes Effective Use of Resources.** The technology to support flipping is increasingly available as schools invest in hardware, bandwidth, and digital content, and as students have greater personal access to powerful mobile devices.

- **Chapter 9: Flipping Builds 21st Century Skills.** Students are using 21st century skills as they use technology to access information in flipped classrooms; teachers use classroom time for activities that build collaboration, creativity, and communication skills.

- **Chapter 10: Flipping the Future.** This last chapter offers pictures of the future of flipping, drawing on thought leaders outside the flipping movement for their views on how flipping may or may not be a means to "flip reform" for lasting educational improvement.

Let's explore this top 10 list in detail.

1

Flipping Maximizes Time for Active Learning

Career and Technical Education

Diane Walters, Sewanhaka High School, Floral Park, New York

Diane Walters worked in the information technology industry for 20 years before entering teaching. She was drawn to flipping because she has always been interested in being on the cutting edge. She teaches in a diverse high school, and her students have a range of academic skill levels and interests. Over the years, she had been frustrated by how difficult it is to keep all members of a class engaged at once. Too often, those who know the material get bored in class and can become disruptive; students at the other end of the spectrum, frustrated by material they find confusing, may also react by disrupting the classroom.

In the summer of 2012, Walters took an online class and learned about blended learning, using mobile technologies and video lessons. It clicked with her: "Many of my students are visual learners. They really have a hard time reading material and extracting information from it. So, rather than assigning more reading, using videos and interactive technologies to reach them just makes sense."

Walters began using video lessons with her 11th- and 12th-grade students in the fall of 2012. She wasn't ready to make her own videos but, like many teachers, found many that she could download from the Internet. Students watch the short (4- to 15-minute) videos at home and answer assessment questions either posed by the video or created by Walters. When they come into class, Walters begins by going over the questions students have submitted about what they saw in the videos.

Then the real work of the class begins: She sets them up to work in teams on a lab activity that challenges them to put into action what they saw on the video the night before—e.g., installing memory in a computer, creating a local area network, or setting up a wireless network.

Her students appreciate the video lessons and are much more likely to participate in class than they had been previously, when she taught the lessons during class. She notes,

> I always had trouble getting through the curriculum in the past. But now I can do in one or two class periods what took three or four class periods in the past. I'm amazed at how fast we went. By the end of the year, I was two months ahead in my curriculum compared to where I was last year. It freed up time to add a whole new topic—computer programming—which was great!

Source: D. Walters (personal communication, June 4, 2013)

This vignette, like others featured throughout this book, peeks into a flipped classroom. Like many teachers at the start of their flipping career, Ms. Walters began by using videos she found online. These, she felt, presented content in a way that her students would understand. But what was important for her was having much more time for students to apply what they were being taught—by doing hands-on projects that demonstrated their competency. The bonus was seeing her students truly engaged and being able to cover more material!

LECTURING: THE OLDEST FORM OF TEACHING

In a traditional classroom, much, if not most, of class time is spent with the teacher presenting content—telling, showing, explaining, lecturing. Whether it's a first-grade teacher reading to students, a high school government teacher lecturing on the Articles of Confederation, or a math teacher demonstrating how to solve an equation, class time is when the teacher delivers information and the students receive it.

Ideally lessons involve a mixture of delivery and discussion, supplemented by activities that engage students to support their comprehension. But in reality, just getting the content across can take most of the class period, especially when lessons are interrupted by student questions, discipline problems, and distractions like announcements on the PA system, fire drills, assemblies, and other disruptions.

There are lots of good reasons for this model and its durability in education. It is an efficient way to assure that all students have access to the same course content, and it provides a way for teachers to transmit their expertise in a subject, and enthusiasm for it, to their students. Most teachers love being the "sage on the stage," and many are very good at it.

Nevertheless, many teachers also feel frustrated by the limitations of this model, especially when lecture and presentation take up the lion's share of the class period, leaving little time for the good stuff of teaching—getting into student's heads, helping them make meaning out of information, drawing out their evolving understanding, encouraging and sparking their excitement and comprehension. In today's environment of high-stakes testing, with multiple standards—and now with the Common Core, new standards—there never seems to be enough time for all the things teachers wish they could do with their students: project-based activities, individual or group learning challenges, deep discussions, and inquiry activities.

So it's not surprising that, when teachers are asked what they believe is the greatest value of flipping instruction, the answer is almost always, "It gives me more time to work directly with students during class." Teachers at Michigan's Clintondale High School claim that, since they have flipped their classrooms, the amount of time they spend with students has increased by a factor of four (www.flippedhighschool.com). That is a substantial gain—and it makes a real difference in students believing that the teacher is there for them when help is needed.

MOVING INSTRUCTION FROM GROUP TIME INTO THE INDIVIDUAL LEARNING SPACE

According to Aaron Sams, "Flipped learning happens when we move direct instruction from the group learning space and into the individual learning space" (Sams, 2013). Listening to information and absorbing it is an individual act, something that goes on in the privacy of one's mind. Why should this be done in the precious, and limited, shared time a student spends with other students and the teacher? Listening to information at home means that valuable class time can be spent doing what happens best in a group—discussing content, making links to prior information, and applying what's been learned.

Graham Johnson, a high school math teacher in British Columbia, puts it this way:

> I agree that video lectures are not new, and sometimes not interesting, but they create more time for meaningful

learning in the classroom I never had time for. For instance, I now have opportunities for journalling, mastery learning, additional math labs, interviews before summative assessments, and my new favourite activity whiteboarding. These are a few of the things I think are moving my practice in the right direction. (Johnson, 2012)

Bloom Would Agree

Proponents of flipped instruction turn to Bloom's taxonomy as a guide for considering the best use of class time. Bloom's taxonomy offers a hierarchical model of intellectual behavior, with those activities requiring ever-higher levels of cognitive skill found at the top of a pyramid (Anderson et al., 2000; Bloom, 1956).

Figure 1.1   Bloom's Taxonomy Revised

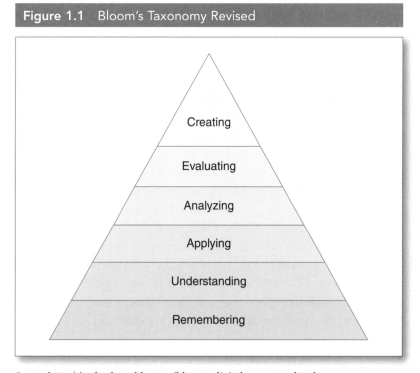

Source: http://techpd.weebly.com/blooms-digital-taxonomy.html

Memorizing facts; recalling information; making sense of it by comparing, contrasting, and connecting to prior knowledge; synthesizing; assessing its quality, value, and impact; and using knowledge to create new ideas, products, and information—all are important skills for learning. These learning objectives build on each other, requiring increasing levels of intellectual activity (see Figure 1.1).

The learning objectives at the bottom of the pyramid (remembering and understanding) are ones that students do best in the "individual learning space," as Sams puts it. It makes sense to move much of this cognitive work out of class time and into the learner's personal time. When this shift occurs, the higher-level cognitive tasks can be addressed in the group space of class activity, where teachers can act as guides and coaches, helping students apply, analyze, evaluate, and ultimately create information. Teachers can apply their expertise, pedagogical skill, and inspirational guidance most effectively in supporting students as they work on these higher-level skills.

WHAT DOES MAXIMIZING THE USE OF CLASS TIME LOOK LIKE IN FLIPPED CLASSROOMS?

How do teachers use the class time, when much of the instructional delivery has been offloaded and moved outside of class? Teachers who flip are adamant that it's not about teachers sitting in the back of the class while students work alone on homework sheets all class period. That would defeat the "conversation conversion" possibilities of a flipped schedule.

There is no one menu, scenario, or playbook for flipped teaching. Flipped classes have varied designs and take many forms, as individual as the teachers that teach them. The snapshots throughout this book offer examples taken from interviews, visits, blogs, and videos shared by all kinds of teachers at all levels. The first shows how elementary teachers use flipped teaching for math instruction with fourth- and fifth-grade students. We'll return to their story in later chapters for several reasons—because flipping in the elementary school classroom is still relatively rare, these teachers are flipping as a team (more on this in Chapter 5), and, as discussed in more detail in Chapter 4, they have conducted action research to evaluate the impact on their students.

Math Instruction

Fourth- and Fifth-Grade Team, Franklin Elementary School, Centennial, Colorado

In the summer of 2012 the fourth- and fifth-grade teaching team at Franklin Elementary School decided it was necessary to do something different to reach students who were falling below grade level in math. Though the school was located in an affluent school district, class sizes were growing—no teacher had fewer than 30 students in his or her class—and the students were all over the map in terms of their learning styles, pacing, and skills. The team had heard about flipping, had read the Bergmann and Sams book, and were inspired to give flipping a try.

They began by determining as a team what the video lessons (usually 4–12 minutes each) should focus on for each unit. They also developed wraparound resources for each lesson: "notecatchers" students were required to hand in at the start of each class to indicate their understanding of the video concepts, and exit slips they'd complete at the end of a class period.

Students are instructed to watch each video at home at least two times—first without stopping, pausing, or rewinding and then, the second time around, to stop, pause, rewind, and take detailed notes on the assigned notecatcher. On the notecatchers students write the vocabulary words used in the lesson, what they learned, questions about the lesson, a representation of the math concept in pictures or other format, and what they see as the link to prior learning.

In class, math periods consist of a 5-minute warm-up activity, 5–10 minutes' discussion of the material on the video and their notecatchers, then 50–55 minutes of guided practice, often in small groups, with lots of conversation. At the end of the class, students spend 5 minutes on their exit slips, which are brief assessments, usually just one problem and an explanation of how they found the answer. (For example, "Explain how to multiply $\frac{1}{2} \times \frac{3}{4}$ using the algorithm you developed.")

Table 1.1 is a summary of how class time has changed since flipping the math teaching.

Table 1.1   Use of Class Time: Traditional Versus Flipped Fifth-Grade Math Classes, Franklin Elementary School

Traditional		Flipped	
Activity	**Time**	**Activity**	**Time**
Warm-up activity	5 minutes	Warm-up activity	5 minutes
Go over previous night's homework	20 minutes	Q & A time on video	5–10 minutes
Lecture new content	30–35 minutes	**Guided and independent practice**	**50–55 minutes**
Guided and independent practice	**20–25 minutes**	Reflection (exit slip)	5 minutes

Source: S. Tierney, N. Heimbigner, J. Maxey, S. Goutell, & J. Melkonian (personal communication, June 7, 2013); Table 1.1 adapted from Bergmann and Sams (2012, p. 15)

High schools teachers are flipping their classrooms in a variety of subjects, with students at all levels. In the public high school in downtown Washington, DC described below, multimedia teacher Melanie Wiscount is excited about how flipping instruction gives her more class time to engage her students in creative projects where they work in teams.

Multimedia Class

Melanie Wiscount, McKinley Technical
High School, Washington, DC

For multimedia teacher Melanie Wiscount, flipping the classroom means her students are using technology as they learn about it. When her class studied augmented reality, Wiscount assigned three videos for them to watch at home to become familiar with the topic. Using the Google form embedded in the school's learning management system (LMS), students brainstormed ideas for historical sites they might use as a basis for an augmented reality mobile app quest they would be creating in class. Wiscount reviewed their homework notes online and used this information to plan for the next day's classroom activities.

In class, Wiscount shared the brainstorming ideas they'd come up with and helped them form groups around common interests and ideas for sites. The groups split into teams, and each team first created a logo for their augmented reality game. For the remainder of class, they worked on the game for the mobile app quest they had selected. There was an active hubbub of excited chatter as they worked, and students were disappointed when the bell rang. Wiscount told them not to worry, the teams were to continue working online at home, sharing ideas and trying out designs on the class site in the LMS. Their work had only just begun.

Source: M. Wiscount (personal communication, May 28, 2013)

Background study at home on their own; discussion, collaboration, and creation in class; follow-up online: it keeps things moving and students engaged, according to Wiscount.

It's not just classroom teachers who are flipping. Many resource teachers also use flipping to maximize the effectiveness of their time with students. For example, media specialists and librarians, often the vanguard in supporting teachers as they work with technology, are also flipping their work with students.

Library Research

Pat Semple, Bullis School, Potomac, Maryland

Librarian Pat Semple started using video when she worked for the local community college. Rather than scheduling group tours of the media center, trying to find times that worked for busy students and faculty, she realized it was much more convenient for everyone if they could learn about the media center through a virtual walk-through on short videos she created and posted on her website.

When she became upper school librarian at Bullis School, a private school for grades 3–12, it was natural for Pat to turn to video. In addition to her class session on using the library, she works with students in all the academic classes to help them with research projects in science, social studies, language arts, even music and mathematics. "They would be bored to tears if I had to stand at the front and do my librarian routine, which many of them have heard every year since the third grade, reviewing basics about the catalog and databases." Instead, she puts nuts-and-bolts information onto short (2- to 4-minute) videos that students can look at whenever they want. The videos cover basic research topics like how to conduct a Boolean search, how to set up a NoodleTools account to create citations and bibliographies, various databases and how to search them, and how to download an e-book from the library. Students watch the videos on their own whenever it's convenient, and they can try things, pause, rewind, and review the concepts as often as necessary. With the basics under their belts, when they come into the library they are ready to get to work on their projects, and time can be spent on the real challenge: research.

Pat likes it because she can now spend most of her time working with students one-on-one or in small groups, getting to know them in a way she'd never be able to if she were just the librarian sitting behind her desk, checking books in and out. In fact, she gives out her e-mail address to students (other librarians are horrified when she tells them this!), so students know she's there to answer questions and provide help, anytime, anywhere. She's opened chat boxes for them to work together at night, on weekends, and even on snow days. "I check my email regularly, and I think it makes them feel appreciated, knowing that I'm there for them. I want them to see me, and all librarians, as approachable."

Source: P. Semple (personal communication, June 5, 2013)

Like other examples used throughout this book, these snapshots illustrate just a few of the many ways teachers are flipping their classrooms to maximize what one teacher calls the "beautiful class time" for active learning.

CAVEATS

Not all teachers in traditional classrooms spend most of their class time lecturing; many have found the time in a traditional teaching mode to creatively engage students in active learning without switching to a flipped teaching approach. Not every teacher needs to flip the classroom in order to engage students. And, typically, even the most ardent flipped teacher flips some but not all lessons.

The project-based learning and in-depth classroom activities illustrated in these vignettes and many flipped classrooms often benefit from block scheduling that allows more time for hands-on work. Even with class time freed from lecturing, flipping teachers can be frustrated with limitations of the standard 45-minute class schedule designed around the traditional classroom lecture format.

Furthermore, teachers don't automatically know how best to apply this freed-up time for learning; it takes time, training, and reflection on what works best with their students. It also requires teachers to be comfortable with classes where creative chaos is the norm. Organizing students into teams, managing their time, and overseeing their various activities requires orchestrating, like a good symphony conductor. Most teachers were not trained for this kind of teaching; many are not comfortable with it.

SUMMARY

• Lecturing has historically been the dominant form of instruction at all grade levels, in all subjects. That's the way most teachers were taught, and it is what students have come to expect will happen in the classroom.

• Moving direct instruction out of the group learning space and into the individual learning space frees up class time for more creative, engaging work with students.

• This shift corresponds to flipping the triangle represented by Bloom's taxonomy, with individual learning tasks (listening, understanding) shifted to the personal learning space, allowing more time for higher cognitive activities (applying, evaluating, analyzing, and creating information) in class.

• Teachers maximize the use of class time in flipped classroom in ways that are as varied as the subjects, grade levels, and teachers themselves.

• Teachers don't automatically know how best to apply this freed up time for learning; it takes time, training, and reflection on what works best with their students.

2

Flipping Facilitates Differentiated Instruction

Eighth-Grade Introductory Biology

Hassan Wilson, Friends Seminary
K–12 School, New York City, New York

When Hassan Wilson began flipping his eighth-grade introduction to biology class in the last quarter of 2012–13, there were definite challenges. Students were moving at their own pace through the material, what he called an "accidental mastery model." Testing, keeping track of student work, and organizing asynchronous labs required constant flexibility and creative solutions:

I have to admit that setting up multiple labs was hard at the beginning, really hard! I had to be very organized. Biology teachers, who frequently work with perishables, understand the difficulty of this task. Imagine placing multiple orders for items, sometimes weeks in advance, some of which have a week or a less shelf-life; imagine doing it in a way that would allow students to conduct the experiment they needed on the day they needed it. Imagine trying to make these projections and accounting for unreliable shipment and students who change their work pace.

Nonetheless, he made it work. He was excited by how lessons sent home on video freed up his time to interact with his students. For example, he found that a presentation on digestion that had taken about a class period and a half in previous years could be presented in a 10-minute video. According to Wilson,

This recovered time was spent answering questions, letting students spend more time on designing experiments, even revising experimental designs and collecting data. I [also] . . . grabbed a few students who struggled and did small group instruction at the board.

Encouraged by his students' positive reactions, Wilson spent the summer preparing to switch all his classes into the flipped teaching mode for the 2013–14 school year.

He reflects in his blog on what he found in week seven:

Students are all over the place—anywhere from one week behind to one week ahead. The number of ahead students has increased in the last day or so. After next week, I plan to speed up the pace a bit and offer more synchronous activities.

Successes: One cool thing that has emerged from post-quiz conferences is pinpointing each student's conceptual issues. In previous weeks, I suggested struggling students to work through pre-planned remediation modules after a quiz. The pre-planned modules are divided into topics, so students always had the choice of how to spend their time. But these conferences have better equipped me to recommend certain tasks or to create remedial tasks on the spot. A few examples will make the point. Two students struggled on the same quiz but had different issues. One student couldn't decipher the difference between codominance and incomplete dominance, while another student had some issues solving blood typing Punnett Squares, which included codominance. For the first student, I told him to create a list of traits (the weirder the better). He had to imagine the appearance of a heterozygote, in situations where the trait displayed codominance and incomplete dominance. I pointed the second student to a blood typing reading and online practice quiz that was already part of the remedial module. I'm also adding more remedial activities to the modules because these conferences are uncovering areas of confusion that I did not anticipate in the planning phase. It would've been difficult to identify and offer specialized remediation without the post-quiz conferences built into the class period, courtesy of the flipped model. My "eduwin" for the week is using post-quiz conferences to suggest tailor made remediation.

Source: Wilson (2013a)

WORKING WITH EACH STUDENT EVERY DAY

Although "maximizing the use of class time" is the most commonly noted reason teachers cite for flipping instruction, reason two is closely connected: Having more time in class means being able to spend more time with individual students, watching them work and gaining the insight necessary to individualize and differentiate instruction. As the snapshot above illustrates, Hassan Wilson found flipping his biology classroom created huge organizational and pedagogical challenges, but it was worth the effort to be able to see students move along at their own pace.

Sheryl Goutell, one of the Franklin Elementary School teachers profiled in the previous chapter, puts it this way:

> The flipped classroom allows teachers the time to work one-on-one with all students. In the flipped classroom, I have actually felt more like a teacher. I have the opportunity to meet my students where they are and guide them to understanding. It is so much more rewarding than lecturing. I also feel like I know my students as learners so much better. I talk to them every day and am able to assess their mastery of each new concept informally. With flipping, I work almost every day with every student. (S. Goutell, personal communication, June 7, 2013)

When students are doing their work in class, actively participating rather than passively listening, teachers have a better window into their skills, approaches, ideas, interests, and difficulties. Some use the analogy of athletic teams: It doesn't make sense for the football coach to lecture on plays and then tell players to go home and practice where he can't see them. A coach knows all of his players' skills, because they are practiced in his presence. Similarly, it doesn't make sense for teachers to lecture in class and then expect students to do the hard work of applying their understanding and practicing alone at home, out of sight and without the teacher's observation, support, and assistance. It's enlightening for teachers to watch their students at work, observing them practice in class what was taught previously. And it is empowering to students to get the help they need before their frustration levels get too high. Just-in-time support, just-what's-needed help—a recipe for everyone's best performance.

Here's how Ericka Senegar-Mitchell, another teacher at DC's McKinley High School, uses differentiated instruction in her flipped biotechnology class.

Biotechnology 1

Ericka Senegar-Mitchell, McKinley
Technical High School, Washington, DC

It's the second half of Ericka Senegar-Mitchell's Biotech I class, made up of 20 sophomores from inner city Washington, DC. In the first half, the class as a whole discussed the previous night's online lesson and reviewed videos that students in the advanced biotech class made, critiquing them and getting ideas for the design of short videos they would later create in teams. Now, using data she's collected from students' earlier work, Ms. Senegar-Mitchell divides the class into groups. Those who have achieved 80% mastery of prior work (Team A) are assigned to the computer station on one side of the class; the others, who need further lab experience to achieve mastery (Team B), work in small groups at the lab station on the other side of class.

Team A students work individually on a series of problems on the class learning management site, digging deeper into concepts covered in their last lab. Team B students work in pairs on another lab activity, "Investigating Enzymatic Rates." Senegar-Mitchell has miniconferences with each pair of students, kneeling down to talk quietly and reinforce key concepts and techniques used in the lab investigation. She notes on each student's checkpoint sheet whether the answers indicate proficiency and whether it was reached on attempt one, two, or three.

For the last portion of the class, the teams switch. Team A moves to the lab stations to work on a new lab activity, while Team B goes to the computers to revisit work they have not yet completed on the earlier assignment. Because the lecture portion of her lesson was sent home as homework, Senegar-Mitchell has time in class for working closely with each of her students, adjusting their learning activities based on their demonstrations of understanding.

Source: E. Senegar-Mitchell (personal communication, May 28, 2013)

FLIPPING AND MASTERY LEARNING

Teachers using flipped instruction are increasingly singing praises for how it offers opportunities to apply mastery learning techniques. Jonathan Bergmann and Aaron Sams call it "Flipped Classroom 201: Mastery Model" (Bergmann & Sams, 2013a).

Mastery learning is built on the work of Benjamin Bloom, of Bloom's taxonomy fame. Fifty years ago, Bloom was frustrated by the reality he found in most schools: Classes moved forward with content when some but not all students were ready (Bloom, 1981). The situation has changed little in schools today. Typically, all students must learn the same material by the end of the unit or lesson; for those who do not, it's too bad—the class marches forward to tackle new content anyway. The relentless demands of the clock and the calendar mean that some children are moved along before they have learned what is needed. Unprepared to tackle the next set of academic challenges, they often fall farther and farther behind.

Mastery learning assumes that all children can learn, given appropriate instruction and time to learn, but that they don't all learn at the same time, at the same speed, and in the same way. It requires a great deal of work on teachers' part to create strategies to address the different learning styles and to adapt instruction to the varying times students may require to master various learning tasks. Teachers create a set of objectives and define a percentage of them (typically 75–80% of all objectives) that each student must meet before moving forward. Regular formative assessments are used throughout the process to ensure that students have mastered each step of a learning task or concept before they move on to the next level. These demonstrations of mastery can take many forms—quizzes, presentations, demonstrations, or even the "hot seat" questioning device used by Canadian math teacher Graham Johnson, profiled below.

High School Math

Graham Johnson, School District 23,
Central Okanagan, British Columbia, Canada

After teaching high school mathematics for several years, Graham Johnson became increasingly frustrated by the fact that many of his students weren't absorbing or retaining information at the levels needed for deep understanding. He learned about flipping in June 2011 when he and a colleague attended a conference in Colorado. They went home and started making videos to use in their classes that fall, becoming, according to the *Globe and Mail,* the first educators in Canada to flip their classrooms.

Johnson set about to create a mastery learning environment using online resources to organize the packages he developed for each unit of instruction. Each unit included a listing of which video lessons to watch and how to access them, text assignments, math labs, and journal instructions. Students could move through each unit at their own pace, as long as they met the test deadlines. Three quizzes were included in each online unit, which students were instructed to take when they felt ready, but results were used for formative purposes, not grades. Students who achieved 70% mastery could move forward; those who did not met with Johnson for remediation.

He recalls, "Before, when I lectured to my class, I figured it was my responsibility to make them learn. And if they were in their seats, that meant they were learning, right?" But he knew it wasn't right. "They had to be learning at my pace, and that didn't work. Some students were struggling, some already mastered the concepts I was covering, and others were tuning in and out." Johnson is blunt in his assessment of testing:

What we did with testing before was a form of "child abuse." We'd make all students stare at a test, full well knowing—as did they—that some were sure to fail. But they all had to take the test, ready or not.

At Johnson's school, math classes are offered in three-hour blocks two to three times a week (it changes from week to week), which means that a student will be in Johnson's math class all morning or all afternoon, with a 15-minute break. Here's how he describes a typical day in his 11th-grade precalculus class:

Students come in and we all talk about where we are, what we did in the previous classes, and I might take a poll on how they think they are doing. We might go over some material or talk about my expectations for where they should be, what will be on the unit test, that type of thing. The students then move into a group activity. These activities are the main reason I flipped my class; they give my students a chance to work on their 21st century learning skills and get their hands wet with the math curriculum!

Following the group activity, the rest of the period is what I call "flex time"—students are free to do whatever they need to get done either alone (watch the lesson video, write in their journal, respond to prompts, take a quiz) or in groups for math "experiments" I've set up for them to do. It's controlled chaos—some kids are working together on problems, some are downloading other videos or lessons, some are even splitting their earbuds and watching my lessons together and asking each other for help when they have questions about the material. At the end of flex time, we spend about 10–15 minutes on debriefing. We talk about how they used their flextime, they summarize their work, ask questions, and I review my expectations for their general timetable for completing the unit work.

I also use their flextime for doing "hot seats" with students one-on-one. That's when I grill them on the content to see how well they understand it. It sounds scary, but the students actually like it. Here's how it works: At the end of the unit students sign up for the hot seat when they think they are ready to take the unit test. Then I do the grilling, they ask questions, etc. From there we decide together if they are ready to go ahead with the unit test for credit, or want to study more, get more help, or work more on mastery quizzes, which aren't graded. They really have to take control of their own learning this way, and it's a terrific way for them to understand their learning progression. (G. Johnson, personal communication, June 13, 2013)

Checking for Mastery by Embedding Assessments in Flipped Lessons

After flipping his class for two years, Graham Johnson began developing a few interactive videos that tailor themselves to a student's understanding. Using flow charts, he embeds questions with real-time responses in the videos. If he's doing a video lesson on factoring, after a few minutes he'll present a question. Students who answer the question correctly then see Johnson saying "Good job!" and are moved to Johnson's discussion of more complex factoring. Students who provide incorrect responses are immediately branched to a different piece of video, in which Johnson says something to the effect of, "I'm sorry you didn't understand. Let me explain that further" and provides a more detailed discussion of the original concepts.

Although all students enter the video at the same point, they may exit at different points. For some students, the video may take just 5–10 minutes, while for others it may take up to 20 minutes to go through, based on how long it takes to demonstrate understanding through the embedded assessments.

Johnson estimates that it takes him up to four times longer to create these interactive videos, but he's excited about how they can become a tool for mastery learning. They don't take away the need for him to work directly with students but rather become a useful management tool for him to use his one-on-one time with each student most productively. He believes that mastery learning is a natural for a building-block subject like mathematics, where, if students haven't mastered one key concept (e.g., basic arithmetic skills), they will never be able to move successfully to the next level. He sums up his approach this way: "Mastery learning is setting students up for success. Before, we were just hoping for their success" (G. Johnson, personal communication, June 13, 2013).

Appealing to Different Learning Styles With Differing Content

Many teachers have found it particularly powerful to offer a menu of ways students can access instruction. Some students may watch the teacher's video lesson, while others might prefer the video lesson made by another teacher in the school, a video from Khan Academy, or a video from any other instructor they find valuable. Still others might find they learn best by searching for the information on the Internet, reviewing a PowerPoint presentation, talking to other students, or even using a textbook! And, when classroom teaching is no longer bound by one textbook, students can pursue a variety of sources. For example, at Clintondale High School, when instruction was put on videos, it was no longer necessary to purchase a textbook for every student. With some of the resulting "found money," teachers were able to select several textbooks from various publishers to use as classroom resources. They, and their students, value having access to multiple resource texts that present concepts and problem sets in a variety of formats, styles, and levels of complexity.

Universal Design for Learning and Mastery Learning

Bergmann and Sams talk about what they describe as the "dark side of mastery"—the demoralizing effect of a student taking a test over and over but never quite getting to the level of mastery necessary to move forward. Clearly, this is a concern that can't be overlooked. Bergmann and Sams found the Universal Design for Learning (UDL) was a useful framework for considering alternative methods of working with struggling students.

Developed by CAST, the Center for Applied Special Technology at Harvard (www.cast.org), UDL recognizes the importance of developing multiple ways to ensure learners of all types have opportunities to easily access computers and other information sources. Early work focused on alternative ways to present information that would meet the accessibility challenges of those with special needs (e.g., visual, hearing, or other physical or learning challenges). The UDL principles have become the technological "learning ramps" that can benefit learners of all types, calling for alternative means of representation (e.g., customized ways of displaying information, use of symbols), action and expression (e.g., varied means of response, navigation, communication, and monitoring progress), and engagement (e.g., optimized elements of choice, mastery oriented feedback, and opportunities for self-reflection) (CAST, 2011).

Applying UDL helped Sams recognize that, although most of his students were comfortable demonstrating their knowledge by taking his classroom tests, he needed to find ways to show mastery for those who were not good test takers (a group he estimated as approximately one quarter of his class). Sams encouraged these students to create their own means of demonstrating their understanding of chemistry—perhaps drawing a diagram or picture, designing an experiment or product, or even writing a song! He was fortunate that his school offered him this flexibility in assessing student mastery and was enthusiastic about how these alternatives to traditional assessment gave him better insight into his students' strengths and capabilities (Sams, 2013).

CAVEATS

Not all schools are supportive of the efforts of teachers to apply mastery learning in their classrooms, requiring instead that all teachers follow traditional and standardized pacing, testing, and instructional sequencing for all students. And not all who flip provide asynchronous, differentiated learning opportunities. Flipped classrooms often continue the one-size-fits-all model of instruction.

Even when schools support mastery learning, teachers who assess student mastery with a variety of formats and approaches within classrooms often become frustrated when their students are still required to take high-stakes tests in traditional formats and at a common time. Flipping won't necessarily change this.

Furthermore, teaching for mastery learning is a skill that takes time and training to develop, and it requires resources (data collection and analysis tools) that may strain the finances of some schools. Schools must invest generously in teacher training, time, and support if they expect mastery learning and differentiated instruction be successful.

SUMMARY

- The second most widely cited benefit of flipping is the opportunity more class time provides for teachers to work with individual students.

- Individualizing instruction makes mastery learning an exciting opportunity, facilitated by the asynchronous instructional opportunities of the flipped classroom.

- Technology (learning management systems, embedded assessments, and data analysis tools) can help teachers with the complicated delivery and management challenges of mastery learning.

- Demonstrating mastery in multiple ways can be a boon for students, but most students are still expected to complete traditional assessments and high-stakes tests, whether or not classes are flipped.

- Teaching for mastery learning is a new approach for many teachers. Training, support, and resources—including appropriate assessments—are necessary for teachers to successfully adopt teaching for mastery learning.

3

Flipping Is Grounded in Learning Theory

AP Chemistry

Ramsey Musallam, Sacred Heart
Cathedral Preparatory, San Francisco, California

Ramsey Musallam is the kind of teacher the kids think is cool. But he is also deeply thoughtful about how the way his teaching impacts his chemistry students. At the FlipCon 13 conference, he described his three phases of teaching.

Phase one was what he called "me blowing things up in class." Here he was, an enthusiastic 23-year-old, jumping around the classroom, totally entertaining. But he was brought up short by his students' honesty in the end-of-the year evaluations. The most memorable was this: "I still have no idea how to balance a chemical reaction but I loved watching you blow %&*! up!"

Phase two came when he started flipping the classroom. This was going to be so great, he anticipated! Using an interactive whiteboard, he made what he thought were powerful videos of his hands working out problems on paper, with a voiceover explaining what was happening. He used multimedia to make even cooler videos. But the student surveys again provided the moment of truth: "Hey, the quality of your videocasts sucks!" Even more disheartening were ones like this: "I can solve all the chem. problems but I hate it when people ask me what it means!"

Why were his students still struggling with actually *learning* chemistry? Musallam realized he was dressing up his teaching with technology but still using the same didactic approaches he always had. It was time, he realized, to change the pedagogy. Reading about cognitive load theory, he recognized that in much of his teaching he was putting far too much information out there for students to absorb. More important, he saw that, for students to focus their cognitive resources on a learning problem, they needed a reason to be engaged with that challenge. Theatrics and flipped lectures may have been entertaining, but they weren't asking anything of the students and weren't engaging them in learning.

Recalling the times when he personally was fully engaged, Musallam remembered how he became totally addicted to the television series "Lost." What was it about that show that held his attention? It wasn't the story line or even the beautiful people on the show. (The acting wasn't all that great, and the characters were not exactly the stuff of Tolstoy.) His "aha" experience came when he realized it was all about the fact that information was intentionally withheld from the viewer. It was the tease, the "mystery box," the big question that drew viewers in and made them want to figure things out based on what they had learned in the last episode. What happens next? Tune in and see if your suspicions are right!

Now in his phase three teaching, Musallam is applying this "aha" recognition to what he calls discovery or inquiry learning. Inquiry learning maintains that it is the teacher's job to stimulate the curiosity of learners by presenting a learning challenge that requires them to activate what they already know, put lower-level information to use, and find solutions that make sense. Now when he flips the classroom, Musallam starts by presenting a challenge in class. He doesn't let students flail around on their own, however; to lower the cognitive load, he directs his students to content they can access outside of class that offers information they need to explore in order to solve that challenge. They come back to class full of ideas; he guides, questions, and nudges them as they work in teams to put the pieces of the puzzle together.

For Musallam, flipping the classroom has become one way to restructure his teaching so that his students have the time (in class and out) and resources (content, each other, and the teacher) to solve inquiry problems that excite their curiosity and make learning chemistry not just fun, but necessary for uncovering what's in that mystery box called science.

Source: Musallam (2013c)

This story illustrates one teacher's personal journey to find ways to embed principles of learning theory into his daily teaching. Like most teachers, Musallam is engaged in a conscious and continuing effort to improve his instructional practice—his pedagogy—in support of student learning.

Pedagogy is defined as "the art, science, or profession of teaching," in the dictionary ("Pedagogy," 1993) but Musallam simplifies it to "the things a teacher does to help students learn" (Musallam, 2013b).

WHAT'S WRONG WITH LECTURING?

Teaching as we know it is typically built on the age-old model of providing information to students through the "stand and deliver" classroom lecture. It's the way most teachers themselves experienced school, and it made sense back when the only sources for information were the teacher and the textbook.

But getting information is no longer the challenge. As Eric Mazur notes in his "Confessions of a Converted Lecturer," with so much information out in the world, the role of the teacher is no longer to transmit information but rather to facilitate students' assimilation of information (Mazur, 2009). Which takes us back to Bloom's taxonomy: Teachers' biggest job today is helping students develop the higher-level cognitive skills of finding, analyzing, applying, and creating information.

Perhaps more importantly, teaching as lecture in many ways contradicts what we know from cognitive science about the best ways to advance learning.

In his "10 Reasons to Dump Lectures," popular blogger and, yes, lecturer (!) David Clark cites what he calls the reasons for, and limitations of, our "deep addiction to the 'hour of learning' delivered as a lecture" (Clark, 2007):

1. Babylonian Hour. We only have hours because of the Babylonian base-60 number system. It has nothing to do with the psychology of learning.

2. Passive Observers. Lectures turn students into passive observers. Research shows that participation increases learning, yet few lecturers do this (Brophy & Good, 1986; Fisher & Berliner, 1985; Greenwood, Delquadri, & Hall, 1984).

3. Attention Fall-Off. Our ability to retain information falls off badly after 10–20 minutes. The simple insertion of three 'two-minute pauses' led to a difference of two letter grades in a short and long-term recall test (Ruhl, Hughes, & Schloss 1987).

4. Note-Taking. Lectures rely on note-taking, yet note-taking is seldom taught, massively reducing their (lectures') effectiveness.

5. Disabilities. Even slight disabilities in listening, language or motor skills make lectures ineffective, as it is difficult to focus, discriminate, and note-take quickly enough in a lecture.

6. **One Bite of the Cherry.** If something is not understood on first exposure, there's no opportunity to pause, reflect, [or] get clarification. This "one bite of the cherry" approach to learning is against all that we know in the psychology of learning.

7. **Cognitive Overload.** Lecturers load up talks with too much detail, leading to cognitive overload. In addition they often go "off on one," with tangential material.

8. **Tyranny of Location.** You have to go to a specific place to hear a lecture. This wastes huge amounts of time.

9. **Tyranny of Time.** You have to turn up at a specific time to hear a lecture.

10. **Poor Presentation.** Many lecturers have neither the personality nor skills to hold the audience's attention. (Clark, 2007)

WHAT MAKES FLIPPING INSTRUCTION DIFFERENT?

The provision of information, even in the form of a lecture, is not eliminated in flipped classrooms; instead, it is generally offloaded to out-of-class time. But when this flip occurs, the information delivery that accompanies flipped classrooms can, if carefully constructed, redress many of the negatives cited above as reasons to dump lectures.

• **Length.** Flipped lessons are shorter than lectures—generally only 10–15 minutes long, so they end before attention falloff can set in.

• **Active Learning, No Attention Falloff.** Flipped lessons allow listeners to pause the presentation, encouraging them to become active listeners. If attention flags, they can always take a break, grab a snack, take a nap, and come back later. And listeners can, and should, write down questions that arise while watching the video lesson, so they can discuss these with the teacher when they are together in class.

• Note-Taking. By teaching students to take notes and pose questions on what they have seen and heard in online lessons, teachers can help students develop critical learning skills that support learning across the curriculum.

• Disabilities. How many students miss what's on the blackboard or demonstrations at the front of the class due to vision problems, or cannot hear or understand much of what a teacher says if they have even moderate hearing issues? Student control over volume, lighting, pace, and even closed captioning in video and online information presentations can provide a real boon to students with disabilities.

• Cognitive Overload and Many Bites of the Cherry. The pause, stop, and rewind capabilities of prepared online infor-mation can address both cognitive overload and one-bite-of-the-cherry issues. Students can absorb content in small bites or chunks, digesting information at their own speed rather than at the speed of the lecturer.

• Time and Location Tyrannies. The tyrannies of time and location are no longer a concern with information sent home for viewing anytime/anyplace that access is available. Given the biorhythms of teenagers, some may be much more alert and able to absorb a lesson at 8:00, 9:00, or 10:00 p.m. rather than in an early morning class.

• Presentation. This final concern—poor presentation—can be as problematic in the video lecture as in the in-person lecture, or even worse. But, as noted above, even a poor pre-sentation in a video lesson is mitigated if the presentation is shorter and can be sped up or rewound or skipped over with-out the knowledge of the presenter. Furthermore, when pre-senters get feedback indicating that certain topics are difficult for students (e.g., how long it took to watch a video, number of times it was replayed), they can edit and improve the online presentation of information.

BUILDING FLIPPING ON A STRONG LEARNING FOUNDATION

Much of the focus on the flipped classroom has been on the video portions sent home. In the homework lessons, teachers try to use (but don't always succeed at using) the best features of video and online resources (e.g., by providing relevant and engaging examples, simulations, graphics and audio components, embedded questions) to minimize the negative aspects of lecturing. But what happens during class time is equally important, or even more so. Does the pedagogy change in flipped classrooms?

It depends. The previous chapters offer a number of creative examples of using class time differently to support active learning. In these examples, teachers are building on constructivist theory, which stems from the belief, supported by research on child development from Piaget, Bruner, and others, that learning is an active process in which learners construct new ideas or concepts based on their current and past knowledge (Bruner, 1960, 1966; Piaget, 1964). It holds that knowledge is constructed during an active process in which the learner is fully engaged.

However, as Musallam found in the example that opens this chapter, just because a classroom is flipped, it doesn't automatically mean students are engaged in active learning. There's much more to it than that.

HOW *DO* PEOPLE LEARN?

How People Learn, the report of a study for the National Academies of Science, provides a useful framework for considering the value-added aspects flipping can offer when seen from a cognitive science research base (Bransford, Brown, & Cocking, 2000). The study suggests four lenses through which to view learning environments: To what degree is a learning environment *knowledge centered, learner centered, assessment centered*, and *community centered*? Let's consider these for flipped classrooms.

Learning Environments Should Be Knowledge Centered

Schools are designed around a shared belief that there are certain kinds of knowledge central to the intellectual development of all students, skills needed for workforce success and the successful negotiation of life challenges, and attributes necessary for informed citizenship. In addition, developing expertise in a particular content area requires exposure to and understanding of a well-organized body of knowledge and tasks in that area, and the development of skills for problem solving and creative work in that particular field.

This knowledge and skill base forms a framework for students to make sense of the many pieces of information, procedures, and processes that enable them to find their way around a discipline and to solve problems in the context of this field of knowledge. As foundational skills are developed, practiced, and reinforced through success (e.g., decoding in reading, applying arithmetic skills, or swinging a tennis racket correctly), the basics become automatic and embedded in long-term memory, freeing up working memory resources for the learner to move to the next level of complexity without having to think about what has become routine (Clark & Mayer, 2011). For effective transfer of skills and knowledge to occur beyond the immediate task, it is necessary that foundational skills and knowledge—including procedures, facts, concepts, processes, and principles—have been well developed and practiced on their own and all together to solve key tasks in the domain.

The Common Core State Standards have defined a set of expected outcomes for all learners across all states and districts. Technology provides a powerful vehicle for sharing teaching in the context of the Common Core standards, and increasingly those who are flipping instruction are creating their own videos, or adopting those created by others, that address the components of the Common Core. Videos posted on YouTube and other Internet sources are providing a window into teaching to these standards. Flipped teaching videos can offer a great resource for supporting the knowledge-centered learning environments at the heart of the Common Core content standards.

Learning Environments Should Be Learner Centered

From infancy onward, humans are always learning. As they become aware of their environment and interact with it, they are constantly building on prior experience and what they've already mastered. When children enter school, they have already developed a personalized set of skills, beliefs, and attitudes supported by a knowledge base, cultural background, and emotional history that all shape their readiness and approach to learning.

In an ideal situation, teachers identify the personal traits and skills of each child, and adapt their instruction to fit each learner's needs, styles, and readiness. But this is difficult with standardized curriculum and timing—the same lessons are given to all students, and all students are expected to complete the same assignments and activities at the same speed. Pacing fits the time of the class period and the school year; the student must learn at the pace of the curriculum, not vice versa.

As was discussed in Chapter 2, mastery learning seeks to provide a learner-centered teaching environment. In a flipped classroom, teachers provide information to students not all at the same time in class (synchronously) but asynchronously, which means lessons can be tailored to an individual student and can be reviewed on the student's schedule. Or if, as is typically the case, just one lesson or segment of information is provided to all students, at least the students can spend as much, or as little, time on it as they want or need, rewinding and reviewing. And, if some students just don't understand their teacher's lesson, they can watch the video of another teacher delivering the lesson, or seek content from a variety of sources that their teacher directs them to, in order to meet their personal learning needs and styles.

Learning Environments Should Be Assessment Centered

Individualizing instruction works, however, only if the learning environment is also assessment centered, meaning that there is regular and timely feedback that monitors progress and confirms deep understanding. As learners meet benchmarks, they can move to new challenges before boredom stifles enthusiasm. For those having difficulty meeting benchmarks, scaffolding and support are needed to minimize frustration and build success. Assessment-centered environments serve as the pacemakers of educational progress.

In flipped teaching, flexible, formative assessments can be provided in a variety of ways. Some, like Graham Johnson, embed quizzes in lectures, so the students themselves can monitor their progress. (See also Stacey Roshan's story in Chapter 6.) Others, like the Franklin Elementary teachers profiled in Chapter 1, require students to respond to a few questions in the online space after viewing the lessons:

- What did you find most interesting in the material?
- How does it relate to what you already know?
- What questions do you have about the material?

This activity helps students develop metacognitive skills—that is, they become aware of their own learning and pay attention to how and why something is known or of interest. Metacognition is a core component of deep learning and of learning to learn, a skill necessary throughout life. For teachers, reviewing student responses to metacognitive prompts provides a window into student understanding and engagement, so they can effectively target in-class activities to students' needs and interests.

Learning Environments Should Be Community Centered

The classroom, school, and broader environments of the family, community, state, and nation are all important for establishing cultural and social norms that impact teaching and learning. The importance of the school as a learning community, in which learners and teachers learn with and from one another, has increasingly been emphasized in the research (Carroll, Fulton, & Doerr, 2010; Fulton & Britton, 2011).

Saying that learning is "community centered" builds on social learning theory, which maintains that learning is not just an individual act, but a process supported by social interactions. Developmental psychologist Lev Vygotsky described a "zone of proximal development" in learners, the jumping off point for further learning, which occurs with the support of those more skilled who act as guides or stimuli helping a learner move to the next level (Vygotsky, 1978). The teacher is naturally one of these guides, but not the only one; learners regularly draw on the expertise of significant others to advance their learning—parents, school and community leaders, and, importantly, other students.

Peer learning is one example of learning in a community-centered learning environment. Many teachers who are flipping their classrooms are using peer instruction during class time. (See Troy Faulkner's use of peer instruction in the Introduction and in Chapter 4.)

Eric Mazur, cited in Chapter 2 for his work in mastery learning, is considered a pioneer in the field of peer instruction. In his college physics courses, seeking ways to engage all students more actively, Mazur broke lessons into segments around core concepts, which students reviewed online as homework. In class, he presented challenges based on the concept; students solved these first on their own and then in discussion with other students. Mazur listened in on the small group discussions, providing support and clarification as needed, guiding students to examine and defend their logic. Following the peer discussions, the challenge or one related to it was presented again for students to solve on their own. The gains in correct responses, for both conceptual mastery and quantitative problem solving, convinced Mazur that peer instruction had real pedagogical power (Crouch & Mazur, 2001; Crouch, Watkins, Fagen, & Mazur, 2007).

INQUIRY OR CHALLENGE-BASED LEARNING

Inquiry learning, illustrated in Musallam's story at the start of this chapter, builds on all four of the how-people-learn lenses. It is knowledge based (learning challenges are developed around core concepts or skills in a domain), learner based (each student brings his or her skill and understanding to the challenge), community centered (students work in teams to solve challenges), and assessment centered (solving the challenge demonstrates understanding). Video content becomes what Musallam calls the "inquiry spackle" to address core concepts represented in the inquiry challenge (Musallam, 2013b).

Musallam believes a student's ability to assimilate information hinges on when the information is provided, which he suggests is best done after a student's curiosity has been aroused. Curiosity stimulates the motivation to learn. Musallam talks about having "the guts to confuse our students, perplex them, and evoke real questions" (Musallam, 2013b). The trick, of course, is doing this without frustrating them or reinforcing any prior baggage that "they're no good at this." Using student questions as guides, teachers can then tailor their instruction in creative and appropriate ways. According to Musallam, "Students' questions are the seeds of real learning—not some scripted curriculum that gives them tidbits of random information" (Musallam, 2013b).

Learning scientist John Bransford and his colleagues at the University of Washington call this approach—presenting learners with a challenge they must explore as a means of learning new skills and information—"challenge-based learning." Their research on challenged-based learning in a number of contexts has shown it to be more effective than learning via lectures (O'Mahony et al., 2012).

And, although flipping is not a necessary component for inquiry or challenge-based learning to be deployed, flipping teachers appreciate how offloading lecture material gives them more time in class for inquiry learning activities. They can then make their homework lessons serve as "inquiry spackle."

OTHER KEY ELEMENTS FROM COGNITIVE SCIENCE RESEARCH

A literature review of flipped learning conducted by the Flipped Learning Network outlines several other key elements from cognitive science research that support the flipped classroom approach (Hamdan, McKnight, McKnight, & Arfstrom, 2013). Three interconnected concepts are priming, chunking, and pretraining to lessen the cognitive load.

Priming

Priming refers to how information is retrieved from memory (Bodie, Powers, & Fitch-Hauser, 2006). Priming is a key factor in learning, because "when learners are exposed to particular stimuli, for example a set of facts, their memory or recall of that stimulus is improved due to their previous experience with the stimuli" (Hamdan et al., 2013, p. 8). When students are exposed to content in a homework lesson prior to coming to class, they are primed to learn the material more effectively when they apply that information in classroom activities.

Chunking

Priming is often allied in the literature with the importance of *chunking* information by organizing small units of information into clusters and putting the clusters together to build capabilities in long-term memory. Chunking enables students to remember more, to access the memorized information more easily, and to deal with greater amounts of information than they would be able to otherwise (Miller, 1956). As they develop video lessons and out-of-classroom information, teachers have recognized that, rather than cover a whole unit that might have once been the basis for a classroom lesson, they are better advised to break the content into smaller pieces, or chunks, that fit what their students have already mastered, with a module or lesson (a chunk) for each new concept. This minimizes the cognitive load, making it easier for students to build up their knowledge in small bites at their own speed.

Pretraining to Lessen the Cognitive Load

This theory holds that if the mental challenge (i.e., the cognitive load) of a learning task is too heavy or complex for learners to absorb at one time, they will mentally shut down. Thus, if a lecture delivered by a teacher in class is too complex or beyond the understanding of some students, they will stumble under the cognitive load and won't be able to carry the information forward. With *pretraining*, as in previewing a video prior to class, a learner can shift some of the cognitive load to the preparation phase—absorbing it in small bits or chunks and reviewing as necessary—freeing up the cognitive resources needed to focus on activities and discussion that lead to deeper understanding when the class meets as a group.

ADDITIONAL AREAS FOR RESEARCH

There are other areas of research that may provide rich fields of inquiry relevant to flipped teaching approaches. Three are noted below.

Synchronizing Audio and Visual Learning to Support Working Memory

Besides being cool, video and audio can offer lots of natural benefits to in-class instruction: close-ups, multiple perspectives, animations, simulations, and the evocative power of music to name just a few. And indeed, researchers have found that instruction that makes effective use of both audio and visual components can lead to learning gains. According to Hess and

Saxberg, nine studies found that "instruction using both text and graphics together—rather than text alone—showed a 1.5 standard deviation gain in learning. Across 20 studies, listening to an audio version of text instead of reading it improved learning by almost one standard deviation" (Hess & Saxberg, 2013, pp. 47–48, citing Clark & Mayer, 2011, p. 403). However, these researchers also note that it's important that the instruction not be cluttered with distracting or irrelevant information; for difficult topics, sorting through distracting information overtaxes working memory and makes it more difficult to learn the important content. This research suggests the importance of thoughtful design of video lessons; a poorly designed lesson that creates cognitive distractions can impede learning.

Learner Background, Learning Styles, and Flipped Learning

Each learner brings her or his own personal history, culture, knowledge, attitudes, and learning style preferences to the educational process. Not all will respond the same way to flipped teaching. Which students benefit most from flipped classrooms and why? Which are challenged, and what can be done to improve their opportunities to learn? How can teachers make flipping more flexible, rather than making it too just another one-size-fits-all solution? These are important topics for further research.

Knowledge Incubation and Consolidation During Sleep

Recent research on the brain has given us new insights into how we process and retain information. One of the most provocative aspects of this research looks at the workings of the brain during sleep. With functional MRIs, researchers have found that during sleep the brain actively processes information that was acquired prior to retiring. It's called "consolidation through mental practice." Research on rats' brains shows that they practice running a maze in their sleep.

Part of the processing of information during sleep involves letting go of unnecessary information that clutters one's working memory, "pruning the day's chaff" to aid memory (Tononi & Cirelli, 2013). For example, I needed to remember that I left my keys on the kitchen counter earlier today. Once I found them, I no longer needed to retain that information and dropped it during sleep, saving space in my working memory for more useful information.

Will brain research provide evidence that students derive extra benefit from the timing of lessons watched in the evening before going to bed? Does this timing help students do a better job of consolidating information, with their brains actively working on lessons during sleep, readying them for the next day? It will be interesting to see how further sleep research sheds light on flipped learning affordances.

CAVEATS

Flipped pedagogy is grounded in learning theory only if it's *good* flipped teaching. As Musallam says, "Flipping a boring lecture from the classroom to the screen of a mobile device is the same dehumanizing chatter, just wrapped up in fancy clothing." (Musallam, 2013a)

As teachers rethink how they use classroom time freed up by sending lessons home, they should carefully consider how they offer those lessons, the formats they use to challenge and engage learners as they watch the videos, and the timing of information for the best uptake on the learners' part.

Whether it be asking students to figure out *why* we put salt on frozen roads and then telling them, creating an environment where students *explore* the features of acid-base titration before sharing the known characteristics, or facilitating the discovery of how batteries work rather than detailing their intricacies, the role of lecture, in particular video, is nothing more than a technique we can leverage. I encourage all educators contemplating "flipping" their classrooms to first detail a path towards meaningful student learning, via a struggle to negotiate perplexity, then inspect their pedagogy in search of useful places to off-load content transfer to video. It is my opinion that placing the "flip" before the pedagogy is nothing but a step in the reverse direction. (Musallam, 2013b)

The science of cognition, like all areas of scientific discovery, is constantly evolving. There is also continuing debate around pedagogical theory, teaching practice, and the role of technology in support of education. If it is to become an established part of teaching practice, flipped teaching will need to be supported by research that provides the pedagogical underpinnings that demonstrate its best use in today's classrooms.

In the meantime, most students have one shot at the fourth grade, or at taking chemistry, or becoming enthralled with calculus. For these students and their teachers, it's now-or-never teaching and learning. But is that teaching working? How do we measure effectiveness? We discuss the topic of effectiveness in the next chapter.

SUMMARY

- Good flipped teaching and learning are grounded in learning theory. When done well, flipping the classroom can address many problems inherent in traditional lecture-based instruction.

- Using the how-people-learn lens suggests that flipped teaching offers opportunities for creating learning environments that are learner, knowledge, assessment, and community centered.

- Other elements supported by learning theory that can be incorporated in flipped instruction include peer instruction, inquiry and challenge-based learning, chunking information, priming learners, and pretraining.

- Processing information through multiple channels of stimuli and learning styles, and using sleep time to process information are important areas for further study.

- The focus of research should be not just on the instructional design or the medium chosen, but on the kind of learning that results, for whom, and why.

4

Flipping Effectiveness Data Show Promise

Schoolwide Flipping

Greg Green, Principal, Clintondale High School, Clinton Township, Michigan

Clintondale High School is typical of many high-need urban high schools: 74% of students are eligible for free or reduced-price lunch, 18% receive special education services, and a majority of students come from minority groups (73% African American). For principal Greg Green and his staff, those factors were no excuse for the fact that too many students were failing, and too many were dropping out.

Business as usual wasn't working. Teachers sent assignments home, and students who didn't understand the content struggled; many just gave up in frustration. It was a vicious circle: Few kids were coming to class prepared, because so few had done their homework assignments. Teachers weren't able to move a class forward when so many students were falling behind.

With the district $7 million in debt over the last 10 years, there was no money to hire new teachers, create smaller classes, or buy new textbooks. Green and his teachers decided to try a different approach: make the informational part of the lesson homework, and then spend valuable class time with students helping them practice what they had learned. The staff began small, beginning with just one freshman social studies teacher, Andy Scheel, who was eager to try flipping. Scheel broke his lessons into chunks, with 5- to 10-minute video lessons as homework, assigned two to three times a week. In class, Scheel helped students as they completed assignments, breaking them out into small groups for discussions and group work.

The results were dramatic: Every student in Scheel's flipped class passed, while the failure rate in a traditionally taught freshman social studies class remained at the same high rate as before. That summer, all freshman teachers were trained to flip, and they began flipping freshmen classes in the fall of 2010. Soon all the teachers in the school were clamoring for training— they didn't want to be left behind. By the end of the 2012, Green and his teachers declared Clintondale High a totally flipped school.

In 2012, Clintondale's scores for 11th-grade students taking the Michigan Merit Exams improved in every subject from the previous year, with the highest gains in reading, where the percentage of students passing rose by 11 percentage points. The graduation rate for seniors, who had only participated in flipped classrooms for a six-month period, rose from 80% to 90%. And, while only 63% of graduates went on to higher education before the school adopted flipping, for the 2013 graduates, the first class to have been exposed to flipped teaching for all four years, a solid 80% were going on to higher education. Table 4.1 indicates passing rates for freshmen before and after the first semester of flipping.

Table 4.1 Percentage of Freshmen Students Passing		
Subject	**Before Flipping**	**After First Flipping Semester**
English Language Arts	48	67
Math	56	69
Science	59	78
Social Studies	72	81

Green notes another positive indicator: "I had teachers say, before, I never once heard some kids' voices in class. It was sad. They never contributed to the discussion." When these same students got help in class, they began to contribute and feel part of the class, which may explain why discipline referrals have declined by 66%.

Sources: G. Green (personal communication, May 21, 2013), Pearson (2013), www .flippedhighschool.com

Clintondale's story has been an inspiration for other schools. The staff admitted they had a problem, but, rather than blame the students, they identified obstacles that prevented students from learning and tried flipped teaching to address these. Although they started small, they quickly ramped up when teachers saw the impact it was having on students. And they collected data, making those data public. Those data tell a powerful story.

THE POWER OF DATA

Having data that show effectiveness is the holy grail in education. Researchers and policy makers in education are hungry for hard data, numbers showing impacts, and, typically, they want it ASAP! In many classrooms and schools that have adopted flipping, teachers have begun to assemble data on grades, testing, and pass rates, but they are cautious about interpreting results too quickly: Educational innovations, especially ones that require a change in teaching, take time to take hold and show an impact.

Furthermore, the issues inherent in school-based research raise important questions that can impact the outcomes: How well were the teachers trained? Whose idea was it, and are all participants really on board with the change? Are the tests the same as those that were used under the previous approach? Do the tests measure the outcomes you are seeking? Is your sample large enough and representative enough to predict that similar results would occur when the same change is replicated in another setting? How much time is required to fairly judge the implementation outcomes? And, bottom line, how much of the change is attributable to the innovation (i.e., flipping the classroom), and how much is due to changes in pedagogy that may have accompanied the innovation?

A Cautionary Tale

A doctoral study of flipping recently posted on the Internet illustrates the importance of these questions (Johnson & Renner, 2012). Researchers hypothesized that students in a high school computer applications class would benefit from the flipped method (when compared with those in a class taught in a traditional manner) due to the change from individuals working on lower-level activities to collaborative group work during class. The researchers found, however, that there was no significant difference in the test scores of students in the treatment (flipped) class versus those in the control classes, nor was there quantitative evidence to support greater student satisfaction in the flipped classroom experience. Teacher questioning strategies did not change, and students in the traditional classrooms actually asked more questions. The study concluded there was no benefit from using the flipped method of classroom instruction.

However, rather than interpreting the data as an argument against flipping, the researchers noted that this was a study of a flipped classroom where the conditions of implementation were problematic. A high school computer applications teacher had been asked to teach two groups of students, with each group participating in a traditional classroom setting for six weeks and a flipped classroom environment for six weeks (a switching replications design). While he taught one group in the flipped environment, he taught the other group in a traditional classroom environment; after six weeks he switched the instructional technique, so each group experienced both flipping and traditional teaching. The researchers compared quiz scores, observed the classrooms, interviewed the teacher, and reviewed student perceptions of instruction based on survey questionnaires.

The researchers noted that there were a number of implementation challenges that may have affected the study results. The traditional class format did not require homework, but, in the flipped class sessions, students had homework—they had to review videos at home. Students had to agree to participate—opt in—and, given a choice between homework and no homework, it's not surprising that not all students chose to participate in the flipped teaching design. Furthermore, two students dropped out of the flipping implementation in mid-course. This meant that, in order to serve these two students during the treatment (flipped) section, the teacher still had to teach traditionally, with direct instruction. This was frustrating to the teacher; he indicated during interviews with the researchers that he wished the flipped model could have been the norm for the class from the very first day. He also stated that each student should have participated in the project, since he was essentially teaching a split class, which made it hard to maintain grading, grouping, and assisting students.

The demands of strict research protocols can adversely impact outcomes in studies like these. In contrast, action research conducted by teachers in their own classrooms is not subject to the same narrow research protocols. These studies can, however, provide important lessons to practitioners. The classroom research undertaken at Byron High and Franklin Elementary schools provide two such examples.

Classroom Data That Tell a More Positive Story

The experience of Byron High School, profiled in the Introduction to this book, tells a very different story. As described earlier, the Byron math teachers flipped their high school math curriculum when it became clear that their old textbooks were no longer matching state standards, and there was no money to order new texts. Starting in January 2010, as the sun was breaking over the nearby cornfields, the math team met from 6:45 a.m. to 7:45 a.m. each Monday morning in their professional learning community. They began the arduous task of literally tearing apart the curriculum and rebuilding it from scratch. The pressure was on; they'd committed to a textbook-free math curriculum for fall 2010.

According to department chair Troy Faulkner, "We looked at the state standards and areas where there were cracks in our kids' mathematical foundations and gave extra attention to those areas." With support from the technology director, Jen Hagan, the teachers created Moodle sites for each course, with lessons, homework, quizzes, and answer sheets embedded in each course site. When they got permission to unblock YouTube, they embedded videos in each lesson and created private channels for each teacher—the better to control what students were watching.

Throughout that first year, they tried to stay a few lessons ahead of the students, adjusting as they went, and they collected data that encouraged them to think that flipping was making a difference. By the end of the 2012–13 school year, Byron's success had been recognized through several national awards, and their story featured in a number of national articles, case studies, and webinars.

The changed teaching styles adopted in Byron's flipped model include a focus on peer instruction, as described in Chapter 3. Thus, although their data show improvement in the percentage of students reaching proficiency through flipped teaching compared to traditional teaching, results were even more dramatic when teachers combined flipping with peer instruction (see Table 4.2).

Table 4.2 Percentages of Students Reaching Proficiency* Before Flipping, After Flipping, and After Peer Flipping

Troy Faulkner's Math Classes, Byron High School**

	Calculus	Precalculus	Algebra 2
Lecture	71.3	74.2	82.9
Traditional Flipping	74.7	80.7	
Peer Flipping	83.4	85.1	94.7

* Proficiency was defined as a grade of 80% or above.

** Data were collected from September 2009 to June 2013.

Source: Faulkner & Warneke (2013)

Action Research at the Elementary Level

The teaching team at Franklin Elementary School, highlighted in Chapter 1, undertook an ambitious action research project to study the impact of flipping their math instruction in fifth-grade classrooms. As noted in that earlier vignette, the teachers were concerned that they were not meeting the diverse needs of all students. They were also concerned that the math lessons took too long, leaving little time for students to practice while in class.

In their action research project, the fifth-grade teaching team hypothesized that the students in the flipped classroom would score higher on the end-of-year test (the Transitional Colorado Assessment Program, or TCAP) than the students taught earlier (before adoption of the flipped teaching approach) had scored. The spring 2013 test results bore this out:

- In 2012 (before flipping), 80% of students attained a proficient or advanced score in math; in the spring of 2013, this percentage rose to 85%.
- In 2013, all of the students identified as gifted and talented scored at the advanced level in math, and another 24 students, not from the G&T cohort, also reached this level. Overall, in the spring of 2013, out of a total of 95 fourth graders, 46 (48%) scored at the advanced level on the TCAP.
- Writing scores also jumped, from 75% proficient/advanced in 2012 to 85% proficient/advanced in 2013, which the teachers attribute to the increased amount of writing required of students as they completed the notecatchers as a part of their homework while watching the math videos.

The team also hypothesized that students would enter middle school "better equipped to advocate for themselves, to actively listen, and to write about their thinking" (Goutell et al., 2012). As one data source for evaluating these skills, the teachers created a form students completed after every unit test, asking students to indicate whether they "own," "know," or "need more help with" most of the learning goals that were taught in the unit. Figure 4.1 indicates the results.

The form also asked students to reflect on how they had participated in the past unit and to set goals for their work in the future. They were asked to circle all that applied in response to the question:

"For me, in the next unit I need to . . ."

The goals that they chose are shown in Figure 4.2. In response to a final question on the unit reflection form that asked students for "additional reflections on this unit about yourself that you would like us to know," the student comments were generally positive, like the following.

Figure 4.1 Students' Assessments of How Well Learning Goals Were Met

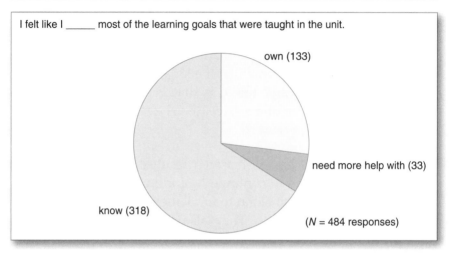

I felt like I _____ most of the learning goals that were taught in the unit.

own (133)

need more help with (33)

know (318)

(N = 484 responses)

Source: Goutell et al., 2012.

Figure 4.2 Students' Learning Goals for Future Work

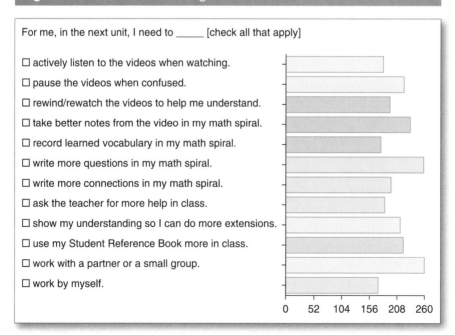

For me, in the next unit, I need to _____ [check all that apply]

☐ actively listen to the videos when watching.

☐ pause the videos when confused.

☐ rewind/rewatch the videos to help me understand.

☐ take better notes from the video in my math spiral.

☐ record learned vocabulary in my math spiral.

☐ write more questions in my math spiral.

☐ write more connections in my math spiral.

☐ ask the teacher for more help in class.

☐ show my understanding so I can do more extensions.

☐ use my Student Reference Book more in class.

☐ work with a partner or a small group.

☐ work by myself.

0   52   104   156   208   260

Source: Goutell et al., 2012.

- "The flip process is helping me because I can rewind the videos, I can't rewind Mr. H."
- "I like the flipped classroom because my teacher can work with little groups to help you understand more, than the whole classroom."
- "I think the flipped math is working for me really well and I like the way that the kids that need more help get extra time and the kids that get it can go strait (sic) [straight] to there (sic) [their] seat and do there (sic) [their] seat work."

Encouraged by the research results, the Franklin team's planned action is to continue flipping math instruction with fifth graders and to begin to implement it with the third- and fourth-grade students. They also plan to work on finding ways to integrate inquiry more into the process, by "creating some videos that encourage the students to think over some ideas and offer some hypotheses when coming to class, instead of always making videos that give the lesson and explain step by step" (Goutell et al., 2012).

MORE TO LEARN

Most K–12 teachers who flip are still experimenting, and most are just one, two, or at most three years into flipping. It's not surprising that the field does not have a robust base of effectiveness data to draw upon. Evidence today relies on classroom teachers' own data sets, like those of the Byron, Franklin, and Clintondale examples cited earlier. As they review their testing results for students in flipped classrooms as compared to results for students they taught previously in traditional ways, the data convince them that the switch to flipped teaching is making a positive impact. For other teachers, surveys showing students like taking charge of their learning in flipped classrooms is evidence enough that it is worth making the change.

Nonetheless, no large-scale external research studies of K–12 flipped classrooms have yet been completed by outside evaluators. One study is in progress; it is being conducted by researchers at the University of Minnesota, who are looking at a pilot project in which teachers used flipped teaching techniques for mathematics instruction for their fifth-grade students in five elementary schools in Stillwater, Minnesota. Researchers in this study looked at student achievement (scores on classroom unit pre- and posttests and on state standardized tests), differences in teaching styles among teachers (through three observations of each teacher), and student attitudes (based on student interviews and online surveys of a random subset of students in the control and pilot classes). Data from this study are expected to be made available at the end of the 2013–14 academic year.

CAVEATS

"Effectiveness" is a big umbrella and means many things to many people. Although teachers' own classroom measures show generally positive results, this may not be strong enough evidence for policy makers to support flipping. And, as noted in our cautionary tale at the beginning of this chapter, many mitigating factors can impact results, making it important to view these studies with a critical eye.

Hard data based on standardized test results—especially state and national assessments—are what policy makers and educators seek as evidence validating the impacts of any new instructional approach. These data are just not yet available for flipped classrooms. More research will be needed to examine in more detail the impacts of flipping on student achievement, along with complementary analyses of how it impacts student attitudes and behaviors, how parental engagement affects student success, and how flipping may facilitate new teaching styles.

One thing is clear: Flipping is making teaching more visible, a topic we discuss in more detail in the next chapter.

SUMMARY

- School and classroom data, collected by teachers and principals at the K–12 level, encourage educators to believe that flipping has had positive impacts on their students' learning and attitudes.

- However, large scale studies that meet strict reliability and validity standards have not yet been completed.

- Research studies are beginning to identify conditions necessary for the successful implementation of the flipped classroom model. These include teacher readiness (training and interest), student and parental readiness for a changed approach, regular formative assessments, and administrator support.

5

Flipping Benefits Teachers Too

Solo Teaching Versus Teachers Learning From Colleagues: Two Scenarios

Traditional Scenario

"Norman" is in his second year of teaching math in a middle school in rural Nebraska. Teaching is a second career for him, as previously he was an actuary at an insurance company. A math major in college, he loves math and wanted to share that excitement with students, so he signed on to a nontraditional certification program for STEM professionals. He soon realized that his six weeks of observation and student teaching left him unprepared for the daily challenge of creating lessons that engage a group of students with varying levels of skill and interest in math.

His predecessor taught this class for 26 years; when she retired she walked out the door and took her lecture notes, and teaching wisdom, with her. Norman had a few visits from the district math coordinator last year, but now, deep into year two, he's still struggling. The other math teachers in his building don't have time to observe his class or help him out, and they haven't invited him to observe their classes. Norman's students aren't making much progress, and he's depressed and frustrated. In fact, he's planning on leaving teaching at the end of the year and going back into the insurance business. His dream of making a difference in students' lives is fading.

Could Flipping Help? Consider This Scenario

Norman and his math colleagues have been meeting together each Wednesday afternoon in a professional learning community to discuss their practice. Norman has learned a lot from these conversations, but he still doesn't get to see how the more successful teachers run their classrooms.

The teachers are concerned that the Common Core standards require a shift in their teaching. The old textbooks just won't work. What to do? They come up with a radical solution: what if they built their own curriculum? With the principal's blessing, they begin to work through the entire math curriculum, first pulling some exemplary lessons from the web, and then eventually video-recording their own lectures and posting them onto the school's learning management system for students to watch at home. They create a common framework for worksheets and problem sets students can work on during class. They regularly check in with each other to see how the teaching is going, dropping in on each other's classes briefly when their own students are deeply engaged. Norman's also been watching the other teachers' lessons online—giving him a window into experienced practice, and they've been watching his and offering suggestions online and in the weekly PLC meetings. He admits,

It's painful to have other professionals see my struggles, but if they can help me do a better job of teaching it's worth any embarrassment. And I really love the sense of collegiality; we're all learning together. It's like working on a team in the business community!

Maybe Norman will stay on next year after all.

Note: Norman is a fictitious teacher, a composite drawn from several anonymous sources.

A TRADITION OF SOLO PRACTICE

The previous chapters discuss how the flipped classroom can benefit students, but one of the most powerful attributes of flipped teaching may be its positive impact on teachers.

Unlike other professions, the cloistered conditions of teaching—one teacher, a classroom full of students, and the door closed—isolate teachers from opportunities to learn from their peers. Like Norman, few teachers have the opportunity to visit other classrooms and see how their colleagues work. According to the MetLife Survey of the American Teacher, today's teachers spend 93% of their workday working alone, in isolation from their colleagues (MetLife, 2009).

Teaching has long been considered a solo practice. One teacher working alone, the king or queen (but hopefully not despot!) of his or her classroom. That one individual is responsible for delivering content and building student understanding of the subject in the ways that she or he believes is best. When that teacher is a great teacher, as many are, the students are lucky and thrive. But when the teacher is struggling, as many others are, the students struggle along with the teacher. With the door to the classroom closed, the students and teacher together suffer through the year without much in the way of alternatives. Parents whose children are blessed with a great teacher consider themselves lucky, but if their children are assigned a novice, unseasoned teacher like Norman, it can be a rough year for everyone.

If Norman could learn by watching or working with that star teacher, it would be great, but teacher collaboration is the exception, rather than the norm, at least in the United States. Our teachers average less than three hours a week in structured collaboration with other educators. Contrast that to the situation in many other countries, where a large portion of educators' paid time is set aside for them to work together and learn from each other. Teachers in the highest performing educational systems spend more time working with other teachers in a week than U.S. teachers spend with their peers in a month (Darling-Hammond, Chung Wei, Andree, Richardson, & Orphanos, 2009).

WHERE DOES FLIPPED TEACHING FIT IN?

Despite the prevalence of solo teaching, the value of teacher collaboration in professional learning communities has been supported by the research literature (Fulton & Britton, 2011). But working together to support flipped teaching is a new wrinkle, one with special potential due to the very public nature of sharing that flipped lessons make possible.

It is not surprising that pioneers Jonathan Bergmann and Aaron Sams staked out the trail to flipped classrooms not by wandering alone in the wilderness, but by working together. Coming to their jobs at Woodland Park High School in the same year, they soon discovered the value of working together to plan their chemistry lessons. When Aaron shared with Jonathan an article he'd found about software for recording PowerPoint slide shows, the put their heads together to explore how they could use this to improve their teaching. They began recording lessons, sharing them, posting them online, and continuing to embellish what they came to call the flipped classroom model. Before long, other teachers saw these lessons on the Internet and began to use their lectures. A movement had begun, by and for teachers (Bergmann & Sams, 2012).

The successful implementation of flipped teaching at Franklin Elementary School, the poster child for elementary school flipped teaching highlighted in Chapters 1 and 4, is likely due to the strong teaching team that worked together as they adopted flipping to improve their collaborative instructional practice.

Teacher Teaming at Franklin Elementary School

Centennial, Colorado

When the fourth- and fifth-grade team at Franklin Elementary School decided to try flipped teaching, their first challenge was creating the video lessons. They considered using ready-made videos from Khan, Learn Zillion, or other online sites, which would have been a lot easier, but they decided it was important to have a direct connection with their students through their personal presence in the video lessons.

They were also aware that, with the introduction of Common Core math standards in the 2014 school year, they had to build their lessons not around any one curriculum, but around key concepts. So in the summer of 2012 the fourth- and fifth-grade team of teachers got together and began creating their own videos. As Sara Tierney says, "It would have really been difficult to do this as just one teacher, because creating the videos at first was a real challenge. But we aligned as a team, and by looking at all our work as a team, it got much easier."

They spent hours and hours that summer, working on their own time and without pay. Principal John Melkonian admits, "I wish I could have paid them a stipend, but at the time I couldn't. But it was their idea and they really stepped up to the challenge on their own power; their level of dedication is truly inspiring."

During the 2012–13 school year, they had regular professional learning community meetings, in which they developed common exit slips for math lessons, analyzed summative assessments to review what was working and what was not, and discussed what needed changing. They also charted all the results on a common spreadsheet. When they saw one teacher's students were doing well in an area where another's students had difficulty, they discussed what the two teachers were doing differently and learned from one another.

Although they had worked as a team before, they really hadn't had time to collaborate or to watch each other teaching—there just wasn't time in the day for that. But in creating the videos together, they talked about various math concepts and how they taught them, and they divided up the creation of videos based on who had a particular interest, comfort level, or approach to a topic. According to Neil Heimbigner,

> The beauty of it is, we all come at it with different angles, and we learned from each other. We each did what we were best at. It was great for the kids to have 6 math teachers, not just one. And some videos we did together, with one teacher asking another a question like "Oh, Mrs. X, I think what you were saying is . . . ?"

Here is an excerpt from the blog they wrote during the first year of flipping, posted by Sara Tierney:

Monday, March 4, 2013

Collaborating as a Team

Now that we are already into March of this first year of flipping our math classroom, I am doing my best to stop and reflect on all that we have learned and achieved this year. One surprising aspect of the flipping process is the relationship we have all created throughout this journey. We were all friends before and respected each other as professionals but there is something about the vulnerability of watching each other teach that really encourages a sense of collaboration and comfort. It was so hard at first to know our teammates would be watching us teach and possibly giving us feedback. And then there is the fact that it's hard not to take it personally when students don't perform well on the problems that you taught the videos on! All of that honest work has made us all so much closer and that much more respectful of one another. We truly work as a team, using data and best practice to drive our instruction. I have always thought I was doing that but this year, WE are truly working as the PLC format is supposed to be done. We have common exit slips almost daily at the end of math time and we share those exit slips, asking How can we help the students that didn't get it? and What do we do with the students that were proficient? Even the process of what to ask the students in the exit slips has been a collaborative process. In the end, we can all agree that we are better teachers, professionals, and friends from this process, and that is something to be thankful for.

Source: S. Tierney (personal communication, June 7, 2013)

CO-FLIPPING: TAKING FLIPPED TEAM TEACHING BEYOND THE SCHOOL WALLS

Team teaching of flipped classes within a school is one thing; flipped team teaching across schools is an even more exciting classroom adventure! One of the most interesting versions of this phenomenon can be found in the flipped English classes cotaught by two high school teachers located on opposite sides of the country. Cheryl Morris teaches in Larkspur, California, and Andrew Thomasson in Gastonia, North Carolina.

Their schools couldn't be more different. Cheryl works at an affluent, high-performing suburban school, where students are focused on getting into top-notch colleges, and parents are deeply engaged. Andrew's school has a mixed population of students drawn from both low- and high-income neighborhoods; at his school, discipline and motivation are regular challenges. Cheryl teaches 11th- and 12th-grade elective English courses; Andrew teaches tenth-grade AP and regular English and desktop publishing.

What unites these teachers are their common passions and frustrations as teachers. After a decade of teaching, both were close to teacher burnout, yet eager to share with students their enthusiasm for literature and great writing, searching for ways to ensure their all their students learned the skills necessary for understanding complex texts and writing clearly. But it was flipping that brought them together.

When they "met" on Twitter, Cheryl and Andrew had each been trying flipped teaching with their own classes for about a semester in the 2011–12 school year. They were attending the 2012 FlipCon conference—virtually—watching sessions online and following conversations on the Twitter hashtag. After the conference, they kept the conversation going about flipped pedagogy and decided to create a video together for something they each taught in their English classes: how to write a good research paper.

> After a few weeks, thousands of direct messages and tweets, a dozen videos, and lots of Google hangouts, we made the decision to team-teach across the country. It may seem crazy, especially as we've never physically been in the same room together, but for some reason, it just works. (Morris & Thomasson, n.d.b)

Cheryl and Andrew finally did meet face to face a year later, at FlipCon 13. By that time, they had been through a year of team teaching, working together in a "backward planning" process that began with the questions,

> "What do we want our students to know or be able to do at the end of the unit? What's the assessment? What will they need to learn to master the content?" Then we start with the major learning objectives and fitting those in to a calendar. Each night, we spend time preparing documents, writing up agendas, recording video instruction, or reflecting on what happened so far in the unit and looking ahead to the next unit. So, basically, we are collaboratively planning every minute of each of our six different

(Cheryl: San Francisco stories, Humanities, and American Literature II; Andrew: English 10 Honors, English 10, and Desktop Publishing) classes. (Morris & Thomasson, n.d.b)

Their students were loving it—having two teachers was cool, and getting to know students from across the country was particularly exciting to them. Andrew's students in North Carolina wanted to know if California really had sunshine every day. Cheryl's California students were intrigued by the Southern accents of their North Carolina peers (C. Morris & A. Thomasson, personal communication, May 29, 2013). And both teachers joke that their students always say they prefer the "other" teacher to their home teacher!

After teaching together for a year, Cheryl and Andrew were convinced that it's not about videos or homework, but rather the "flipped mindset" of putting students in the center of instruction (see Introduction). They would be the first to say it's not easy. But they are energized by the process and how they learn every day from each other. They are also sharing their experience with others through the Flipped Learning Journal (www.flippedlearningjournal.org), which supports a weekly chat and a space for collaborators to meet (the Co-Flip Collaborative) and share their stories of coteaching.

Their philosophy is best demonstrated by their answer to the question, "Can I flip my class by myself?":

You can, but we wouldn't recommend it. Unless you're a total fan of exhaustion and burnout. Or a robot. Excitingly enough, individuals around the Internet have been collecting lists of Flipped Classroom practitioners for some time now, and we're happy to be able to share those with you here (www.flippedlearningjournal.org/forms-for-flipped-community.html). Better yet, fill out the subject-specific form that most applies to you on this page (www.flippedlearningjournal.org/forms-for-flipped-community.html) to add yourself to the lists! Many of these people could also use a collaborative partner. Contact them. We're always better together. (Morris & Thomasson, n.d.a)

TEACHER LEARNING: EMBEDDED AND FLIPPED PROFESSIONAL DEVELOPMENT

Teachers learning from each other. Is this an accidental by-product of flipped teaching, or is it at the core of the flipped philosophy? One thing is clear: When teachers record their lessons on video and post them online, they open the door to their classrooms. It doesn't have to be across the country like Morris and Thomasson. For some, using a school network or password-protected link, their lessons are open only to other teachers in their school or district, but even that is a huge change from normal practice. Some schools actively encourage teachers—and their students—to view the videos of other teachers. For the students, it is another learning resource. For teachers, it has become a new kind of embedded professional development.

Working together to develop their revised math curriculum created a bond among the math educators at Byron High School. At the conclusion of this intensive nine-month effort, they had created a full library of lessons on YouTube. Students are invited to watch any teacher's lesson since, even if a course is taught by several teachers, it is built around the same curriculum and tests. Most students prefer to watch their own teacher, but some have found that, if there's a concept they have a hard time understanding, it can help to see another teacher's take on explaining it. And the teachers themselves realized early on that, by watching each other's videos, they could see other ways of presenting concepts, and they often revised their teaching as they benefited from new approaches or techniques they borrowed from one another.

Byron math teacher Rob Warneke is comfortable with this openness:

> If my kids don't get it from my lesson, they have access to Troy's, Darren's, or Jen's (the other Byron math teachers) videos. We each have our own style, so they may want to

watch all three. If I'm bombing out on a section and I see that my way of presenting a concept isn't working, I'm going to watch Troy's video to see what he is doing. Even with my class right down the hall from his, we just don't have time in the middle of the day to get together and talk about it. But I can pull up his video at any time and take a look to see what he did that I might want to consider. (R. Warneke, personal communication, October 2011)

Teachers learning from watching video lessons on their own time; stopping, pausing, replaying, taking notes; then discussing what's been learned when together in a PLC or staff meeting. Sound familiar? Sounds like flipped professional development to me.

Flipping Formal Professional Development Coursework for Teachers

Other forms of educator professional development can benefit from flipping to better utilize teachers' valuable time. External courses educators take for college credit or continuing education units, as well as school- or district-led courses required for school reform or improvement efforts, are increasingly being offered in a flipped format.

Flipped Professional Development for New Teachers

Dan Tripp, Parkway School District, Creve Coeur, Missouri

The new teacher induction program for the Parkway School District requires novice teachers to participate in 12 hours of district-led professional development in each of the three years prior to receiving tenure. Previously, all teachers had to come together for two-hour sessions held six times a year, but in 2012–13, staff development facilitator Dan Tripp decided to try something new. Rather than spend each two-hour session presenting information, Tripp created a series of videos in which key components of the topic (assessment literacy) were compressed into short (5- to 10-minute) videos. The novice teachers could watch the videos on their own time, testing their understanding before moving to the next one by answering short quizzes embedded in the videos. Then, when they met for the group face-to-face sessions (which were now cut to one hour), they could spend their time discussing what they heard, sharing examples of how it related to their teaching, and writing assessments based on the principles they learned. The teachers loved it—with 94% indicating they prefer the flipped professional development.

Source: D. Tripp (personal communication, November 4, 2013)

Flipping professional development makes smart use of scarce time and resources for teacher learning. It also is a way for teachers to experience firsthand what flipped learning is like—a good introduction to flipping their own teaching.

ARE TEACHERS READY TO USE TECHNOLOGY FOR FLIPPING?

In the past, technophobia and lack of skill were blamed for teachers' reluctance to experiment with new ways of teaching that could be supported with technology. While this may remain true for some teachers, the picture has changed dramatically in the last few years.

As we discuss in Chapters 6 and 8, there's a large installed base of technology available to teachers in most schools today. Furthermore, many young teachers are themselves digital natives, comfortable embracing digital resources. According to data collected by PBS Learning Media for the national 2013

Digital Learning Day, nearly three quarters of all teachers (74%) said they use digital resources to expand or reinforce classroom content. One of the most common kinds of digital content cited was online lesson plans; 48% of preK–12 teachers use them (PBS, 2013). According to Project Tomorrow's 2011 survey (Project Tomorrow, 2012a), 65% of teachers reported that they create and upload videos, music, and photos, and 54% create multimedia presentations. As teachers master the skills necessary for developing flipped lessons, and as the technology becomes easier to use, a small number of teachers have taken the next step: creating their own videos for flipping their classrooms. The 2011 Project Tomorrow survey data show that 15% of teachers surveyed say they create videos of their lessons or lectures for students to watch (Project Tomorrow, 2012a).

Teachers are also using the Internet to learn from one another. In 2008 less than a quarter of all teachers (22%) maintained an online social network for professional reasons, but by 2012, half (52%) of those surveyed said they were keeping a social networking site updated. Growth in teacher participation in online professional learning communities has also been rapid, with one in three teachers reporting that they participate in online professional communities. As discussed earlier (see Introduction), in the fall of 2013 there were over 16,000 members of the professional NING sponsored by the Flipped Learning Network. The number of blogs, websites, webinars, and other sources of formal and informal learning is expanding daily. It makes it less intimidating for those contemplating new forms of teaching using technology—like flipping the classroom—when you have a community of peers out there ready, willing, and eager to help.

CAVEATS

Are we going back to solo teaching and flipped superstars? Remember Norman? For him, the process of creating a flipped classroom wasn't so much a way to teach differently but rather an opportunity to learn with and from other teachers. But if educators use this resource to showcase superstar teachers who work in isolation—or to promote those whose "super videos" can be used (or purchased) by teachers without changing their own teaching, we may be missing the boat.

Might "open" classrooms create risks for teachers? The short answer is yes. In an era when teacher evaluation is a hot topic, and teacher observations are one component that goes into critical decisions on teacher tenure, promotions, and merit pay, those who don't "show well" might well face the risk of negative consequences. Transparent teaching must be accompanied by an environment of trust, where teachers have the freedom to fail and learn through those failures. Teachers need to be able to work in an environment where the learning and sharing that come with open-door teaching will be viewed by all as a learning experience, not an opportunity to find fault or punish failure.

Teacher time is a valuable underreported resource. Teachers report that finding, reviewing, and making teaching videos is a huge time commitment. Some also make themselves available to students (and parents) out of school hours (via email or text) to answer any questions that arise. These burdens are not to be taken lightly and may raise concerns with unions if teachers believe their compensation does not match their extra efforts.

Intellectual property and teacher-produced videos. Ever since teachers have been able to share their lesson plans by posting them on the Internet, the question of intellectual property has been a concern. The typical teacher inclination is to share what they do—and, with the growth of educational commons (e.g., YouTube, TeacherTube, Learn Zillion, and others), the audience for good online lessons is vast. However, there is a new commercialization of teacher videos, and this troubles some teachers:

I put my videos on iTunes, YouTube, wherever it is easiest for my students to access them. That means they can be viewed by educators all around the world—and used by them. I get fan letters from other teachers. I like that! Sometimes even students contact me and say they wish their teachers would use my videos instead of making their own! I couldn't be happier to have other teachers use my videos if it helps students learn. But some teachers are taking their videos down and selling them—or their school districts are selling them to other districts. That just doesn't seem right to me.

It is ironic that the growing popularity of flipping has meant that what began as a grassroots, bottom-up teacher movement has now become big commercial business. As more teachers look for high quality content—for flipping or as additional resources in their teaching—the videos created by teachers are becoming part of the marketplace of teaching resources valued by publishers and professional developers. Will what was once free become yet another commodity? And shouldn't teachers be compensated for their efforts, not to mention their talents?

Might teachers become obsolete? Some critics worry that good teachers could be replaced by great videos. (Or, worse, great teachers might be replaced by mediocre videos!) In higher education, massive open online courses (MOOCs) have captured the excitement of those seeking to expand access to high-quality instruction at little or no cost. The implications for higher education are huge. We are just at the stage of crystal ball gazing in terms of predicting how this model—top teachers and teaching available to all students, anytime, anywhere—will translate to preK–12 schooling. As the capabilities for online, blended, and video teaching advance, both positive and negative implications for teachers and the profession of teaching must be considered. We discuss these issues further in Chapter 10.

SUMMARY

• Flipped classrooms can benefit teachers and their learning as much as the learning of their students, especially if schools use the process and products of flipping as a tool for showcasing, analyzing, and improving teaching in a collaborative, supportive environment.

• When teachers work together in creating videos and analyze them as "input data" they correlate with student outcomes, flipping can be a powerful form of professional development.

• Flipped professional development, in which content is viewed prior to teachers meeting together as a group, makes effective use of scarce time and resources for teacher learning.

• Teachers today are increasingly comfortable using technology and have a growing base of technological resources to help them learn about flipping (or teaching in general) from one another.

• As more teachers edge toward flipping their classrooms, an environment of trust must surround this work. Unless teachers have permission to fail as they experiment with new approaches, they will be loath to risk opening their classroom doors to others.

• The changing role of the teacher in the flipped classroom, discussed more fully in Chapter 10, is a critical topic for discussion among teachers, administrators, policy makers, and all who care about the future of education.

6

Students Like Flipping

A Student's Take on the Flipped Classroom

Harrison Mendel, Okanagan Mission Secondary School, British Columbia, Canada

Student-created videos are among the most powerful testimonials to why flipping is so attractive to kids today. One created by Harrison Mendel, then a tenth-grade student in his second year of flipped classrooms, shows a day in the life of a flipped student (http://www .youtube.com/watch?v=dLcO6zZdOyw). Using no narration, just video, text labels, and background music to set the mood, this short video makes flipping seem like a normal way of learning, far preferable to the traditional classroom model.

Our young man begins his day checking out a lesson on his laptop while eating his breakfast. He slips his laptop into his backpack (no heavy books for him) and boards the school bus. In school he talks with a teacher who is concerned about the amount of time the young man has been absent. The teacher notes that he's gotten behind the rest of the class but reassures him, "Watch these videos and I think you'll be able to catch up." Cut to the student opening a laptop, watching the recorded lessons on his own, and then working on his math problems in class with a teacher at his side, who coaches him as he talks about his work.

The video then switches to preflip frustration: Another student, frustrated by math problems she is working on for homework but doesn't understand, angrily crumples papers, breaks pencils, and throws them against the wall. But after she watches a video lesson in the quiet of her home, she texts her friend, "I think I get it now. These videos are cool."

Subtitles under these images tell the students' messages: "never miss a lesson," "teacher interaction," "relearn concepts." The students in the video use whatever they have to watch their flipped lessons—tablets, phones, laptops. They handle them with the speed and dexterity that comes from hours spent texting, searching, downloading. It's their world, and they are happy to welcome teachers to it!

Source: Mendel (2012)

One of the most widely accepted beliefs about flipping is that students love it. Less time spent spinning their wheels when they don't understand the homework, fewer heavy books to carry home in a backpack, opportunities to move at their own pace, not falling behind when sick or out of class for extracurricular activities, using technology—what's not to like? Even those who have never experienced a flipped class like the idea. According to the 2013 Speak Up survey, almost three quarters of middle and high school students surveyed think flipped classrooms would be a good way for them to learn (Project Tomorrow and Flipped Learning Network, 2014).

USE OF TECHNOLOGY IS NOT JUST COOL, IT'S EXPECTED

Today's students, whose first cries were captured on phone photos and relayed instantly to loved ones around the world, are digital natives in every sense of the term. Born after the infusion of the Internet into daily life, they are indigenous digital learners, active digital communicators, enthusiastic digital creators. Tweeting and texting, gaming and Googling, friending and Facebooking, most young people today are comfortable using technology for all aspects of their daily lives. It's as natural to them as eating and sleeping (and often interferes with these and other daily activities!).

Data from the Speak Up 2012 survey of 364,240 students, K–12, provide a picture of students' uses and views of technology for schooling (Project Tomorrow, 2013a):

- 75% of K–2 students who responded to the survey said they use computers and mobile devices to play educational games on a regular basis.
- One third of respondents in grades 6–8 said they'd prefer to read a digital book for school work, and for personal reading, 41% of those surveyed preferred to read a digital book.
- Over 50% of respondents in grades 6–12 said they use the Internet to help with homework at home at least weekly, and 29% of high school students use it on a daily basis.
- 38% of student respondents regularly use Facebook to collaborate with classmates on school projects.

According to the most recent Speak Up Survey, almost a quarter of students (23%) are accessing videos created by their teachers, and one third are accessing online videos on their own to get help with homework (Evans, 2014).

For this generation of students, using technology in schooling is a natural. When they do not use technology in their classes, it makes school even more disconnected from the real world and the things they find important. And, as we discuss in Chapter 8, many now have the technology available to them. At the time of the 2013 Speak Up survey, 89% of high school students, 73% of middle school students, 50% of students in grades 3–5, and 22% of K–2 students reported that they were smartphone users (Evans, 2014).

Many administrators have seen the wisdom of supplementing school-provided technology with students' personal devices. In 2010, just one fifth (22%) of principals were willing to allow students to use their own mobile devices at school for academic purposes; by 2012 this figure had jumped to over a third (36%) (Project Tomorrow, 2013b). For many students, the technology they know and love, and carry with them everywhere, is a natural vehicle for their learning. In fact, in describing their ideal school in the 2013 Speak Up survey, 62% of students said they wish they were allowed to use their own devices at school (Evans, 2014).

SELF-PACING BRINGS INDEPENDENCE TO LEARNERS

High school physics teacher Kathryn Lanier describes what she sees as greater student independence and other benefits students derive from participation in her flipped classroom (Lanier, 2013):

> Students become more responsible for their learning. They are expected to arrive with some exposure to the topic and the willingness to try to apply the new knowledge. . . . The students who catch on to a topic quickly could move into the work portion of the class and often finish. When finished they could start the work for the next day, do an extension activity of their choice, or work on some other work. Students who struggle with math or problem solving are given more time and assistance working with the problems without the pressure of moving on with the entire class. Problems, activities, and labs are no longer frustrating for the students as they can get the help and explanations they need exactly when they need it while they are working.

Many teachers who flip their classrooms survey their students for their reactions, and use these results to refine and hone their approach. Graham Johnson, the British Columbia high school mathematics teacher profiled in Chapter 2, took this one step further when he made a study of student perceptions of his flipped classroom the subject for his master's thesis. His results indicated that a majority of his students enjoyed the flipped classroom (only 8% found it less engaging than a more traditional classroom, and just 7% said they would not recommend the flipped classroom to others); they were spending less time doing homework (perhaps a reason for the positive reactions to the change!); and they found the videos beneficial to their learning (Johnson, 2013).

As Johnson found, students respond positively to the challenge of independence and responsibility that comes with self-pacing. What seems to be empowering is the autonomy they are given—along with which much-needed privacy when they are having problems—as long as it is supported by quick and personal feedback by the teacher. Self-pacing can be a boon to students who find themselves painfully aware that they are not keeping up with the class. No one wants to be the one who is holding the rest of the class back. At the other end of the scale, for those achieving at faster and high levels, the opportunity to move at a pace that works for them is a refreshing option that can be extremely motivating.

Jennifer Green, one of the high school math teachers at Byron High School, surveyed her students about how they felt about her flipped classroom. The comments she received are typical of what many students say, once they have become comfortable with the flipped classroom:

> I was gone on a trip and missed three days. Having the video online assured me that I was seeing exactly what everyone else in the class was seeing and there was nothing else I was missing.

I like that I could get through the video lesson faster at home, and I feel I learned the info better [because] I could just listen to it by myself. By having all the class time to work on homework I can ask questions and work with other people when I need help.

We don't have to waste time in class learning everything. I also liked that you can take notes and learn at your own pace.

I like being able to rewind the lessons and pause them. It gave me more time to think about things and work through them without being rushed. I like the fact that I can rewatch them if I have questions. I like being able to do my homework in class because then I can ask more questions as I go along. It also takes less time when I have help right away instead of struggling through it on my own. (Green & Fulton, 2013)

REWINDING THE TEACHER

Elementary-level students have many of the same reactions to flipping that their high school peers have. One of the most common benefits they cite is being able to "rewind the teacher." At a panel of fourth-grade students engaged in the flipping pilot in several elementary schools in Stillwater, Minnesota, the students talked about how excited they were when the teacher showed them how to get on Moodle, how they could rewind parts they didn't understand, and how class time was different: "We could do math experiments." "If I don't understand I can ask teacher." It was "way helpful for teachers to help us more."

MORE STUDENT ENGAGEMENT = FEWER DISCIPLINARY PROBLEMS

Students' positive reactions to a more student-centered classroom have been reflected in teachers' reports of a drop in disciplinary problems when students are more engaged with the work (as described by Diane Walters in Chapter 1 and Greg Green in Chapter 4). In the teacher-centered classroom, with a teacher lecturing and all eyes (expected to be) focused at the front, there is also more bang for the buck for a disruptive student; distracting the lecture by capturing the whole class's attention takes less effort. But when a teacher is no longer lecturing to the whole class, but rather moving around throughout the room, with students working independently in small groups, the class clown or loudmouth has a much smaller audience for his or her buffoonery or inappropriate comments. Even if the flipped class can seem louder and more chaotic to the casual observer, it is often a busy, creative buzz indicative of the kind of engagement that means learning is indeed taking place!

MORE TIME WITH TEACHERS

Spending more time with individual students is seen as a huge plus for teachers. Kathryn Lanier says that while students are working in small groups or independently in her classes, "There is plenty of time to interact with each student many times during a 90-minute period" (Lanier, 2013). Graham Johnson uses some of his class time for the "hot seat" interviews with individual students to assess whether they are ready to take the unit tests. And the teachers at Carbondale High School estimate they are now spending four times more time with each student than they have in the past.

Teachers think this extra interaction is terrific, but what do students think? Most students in flipped classrooms like having more personal time with the teacher, but for some this may be a double-edged sword. It is much easier to hide when the teacher is in front of the class lecturing, and you are sitting in the back napping or doing your own thing. For some students, this alone is reason enough to admit to having mixed feeling about their flipped classrooms!

NOT ALL STUDENTS WANT TO ADJUST TO A NEW TEACHING STYLE

Watching a lesson on a video is not a big deal for most students; the tricky part is adjusting to a new teaching style and learning the best ways to learn with and from online lessons. Many students have learned to "play the game" of school, and play it well, especially by the time they reach high school. They are used to sitting back and listening to lectures (or tuning them out) and expect information to be delivered to them. Rightly or wrongly, being passive can be cool and saves energy for the important things in school—sports, extracurricular activities, and social life. Students have built a repertoire of school skills that have served them well in the past. It can be unnerving when teachers change the game and expect them to adapt to a new approach, one that puts more responsibility into their own hands.

When teachers survey their students soon after the introduction of flipping, this discomfort with change is often apparent. The reviews can be harsh, but fearless and dedicated teachers like Hassan Wilson, the eighth-grade biology teacher from New York profiled in Chapter 2, use such reviews to guide their thinking about what worked and what needs to be changed in the future. After he tried flipping in the last quarter of the 2012–13 school year, Hassan was encouraged that the anonymous surveys he asked students to complete indicated that the majority of his students liked the model, with comments ranging from the cheery "I really liked it" to the more guarded "It took a while to get used to . . . however it was fine."

But he was concerned that a few clearly did not like the change. Their comments were blunt:

I didn't love that model, because sometimes I would have questions about the lesson but I would forget to ask them the next day.

I did not like it at all. I found it confusing and harder to learn the stuff.

I would prefer to do the written work at home because if I learn things at home, I cannot ask Mr. Wilson about any confusing material.

Like a customer satisfaction survey, Wilson used the responses to improve his product: his teaching (Wilson, 2013b).

Preparing Students for the Flipped Classroom

Teachers like Wilson have learned that it's important to prepare their students carefully for what they will experience in the flipped classroom. Time spent up front, helping students transition from a teacher-directed classroom to the more student-directed activities necessary for success in flipping, is time well spent. For example, although it may seem intuitive, students need to be reminded that they can pause videos and rewind if they don't understand something—and that they can also can run it forward and skip areas they already understand. Wilson also found that students were not prepared to take notes on videos that first year, so he spent more time preparing his students with note-taking techniques in the 2013–14 academic year.

This kind of student preparation was carefully orchestrated by the fifth-grade teaching team at Franklin Elementary School, as described in Chapter 1. Like her colleagues, Sheryl Goutell introduced her elementary students to flipping very gradually. Students were first taught how to take notes, and then instructed on how to watch, pause, and rewind the videos.

Do Students Actually Watch the Video Lessons?

How can a teacher be sure students watch the videos? Some teachers have embedded questions within the videos or provided forms for students to complete online prior to class. Reviewing the online responses also helps the teacher plan how much time in class should be devoted to a review of the material and which students need that assistance.

This is the approach taken by Stacey Roshan, a high school math teacher at Bullis School, the school profiled in Chapter 1. Roshan realized that her Algebra 2 students were nervous at first about her class, as for many this was their first really hard math class. It was a heavy load of information and new ideas to absorb at first, and the class lectures had often been overwhelming to them in the past. But when she sent her class lectures home, many students reported that they found it much easier to watch the 10- to 15-minute videos, because there were no distractions, and they could really focus without interruptions. According to Roshan, "Students were relieved to be able to have both me and their classmates there to help during the problem solving activities versus having to go home and work through difficult problems alone" (S. Roshan, personal communication, June 5, 2013).

Roshan began to embed short quizzes (multiple choice, short answer, fill-in-the blank, or true/false) in her videos for several reasons. First, of course, they gave her a way to be sure students had watched the lessons. The online quizzes told her how well the students understood the lesson, and she used the results to plan the next day's activities. But the software she used also gave her useful data, telling her how long each student took to watch the video and how many times students rewound and in what places, as well as how long it took them to take the quiz. She noted, for example, that one of her students watched every night's lecture twice. "She was a hard worker and knew that she was going to have to put extra effort into the class. Her work ethic was fantastic, and she learned so much that year" (S. Roshan, personal communication, June 5, 2013).

Roshan comments, "It's been amazing to see how far my students have come in terms of independence. They've taken responsibility for their own learning and are learning how to ask good questions." That makes the discussions in class much richer, as asking good questions is a skill that is often overlooked. She's also really pleased at how the anxiety level has dropped since she started flipping lessons. Her students know they have lots of time to watch lessons, even if they don't understand the material first time around (S. Roshan, personal communication, June 5, 2013).

CAVEATS

There is no one-size-fits-all solution to teaching. Every child is different, and flipping may not be for everyone. It's important for teachers to monitor the impact that any new teaching style has on each student; to assess who is thriving, who is coasting, and who is not doing well; and to determine what can be done to help students who are floundering. If the presentation and material aren't matched to a student's readiness level or ways of understanding, the student may not engage with the lessons posted online any more than he or she engages with lessons delivered in class.

All students need time to get used to the flipped classroom experience. There is a learning curve involved that teachers need to take into account.

Students will fall behind if they are not following classroom lectures assigned as homework. They need to understand that there are consequences for falling behind, just as there are consequences for not doing homework. As one teacher noted, "If a student hasn't watched the video, they quickly learn that they are going to miss out on the cool things we do in class. They have to go back and watch it before they can participate. That's a pretty strong incentive."

Furthermore, although students may be attracted to the novelty of flipped classrooms today, they may be just as likely to grow bored with this approach once the novelty wears off. What was new and cool today can seem old fast to students for whom technology represents rapid change and ever new and evolving features, bells, and whistles.

SUMMARY

- Students use technology in all aspects of their daily lives, and they expect—and want—to use technology more in school.

Because they are comfortable communicating, finding information, and creating with technology, most are primed for the ways that technology is used in flipped classroom models.

• Many (but not all) students in flipped classrooms respond positively to the independence and responsibility for their own learning required in flipped classrooms.

• Preparing students carefully is important, as the switch to flipping is not an automatic one. Certain techniques (pausing and rewinding and taking notes on videos, crafting questions to ask in class about the content, checking oneself for understanding) are critical for success in out-of-class learning.

• Students generally view having more time with teachers as a plus, but it also means less chance to hide at the back of the class! Also, some students are frustrated by not having the teacher beside them to answer questions that arise in watching lessons out of class.

• Like any teaching technique, one size does not fit all. Because student reactions and adjustments to flipping are variable, teacher monitoring of each student's ability to adapt to the flipped classroom is critical.

7

Flipping Brings the Classroom to Parents

School Looks Different!

The video "Showing the Difference Between a Traditional and a Flipped Classroom" (http://flippedclassroom.org/video/the-traditional-vs-flipped-classroom-an-ap-physics-example) provides a humorous but useful contrast between the traditional classroom and one where flipped teaching has been adopted. For most parents, the "before" image is what they recall: the teacher lecturing at the front of the class, writing formulas on the board (even if it's a whiteboard now instead of the blackboards they grew up with). It's neat and orderly, students sit in rows, and all that quiet must mean learning is going on. Right? But as this video shows (and as demonstrated in many other videos posted by flipping teachers), in the "after" image, the classroom looks very different: There's lots of noise, students are working in groups, there's lots of action, and one really has to look hard to even find the teacher! (He's huddled with a group of students, watching them do the lab work they'd reviewed in the previous night's video homework.) And what kind of homework is watching videos anyway? Whatever happened to worksheets?

PARENTS' VIEWS OF CLASSROOMS: MEMORIES OF BYGONE DAYS

Parents have clear images for what they expect in a teacher and a classroom, images formed by their own experiences during the years when they were students. Everyone went to school, so everyone knows education, right?

These memories from our days of schooling are so deeply ingrained in our collective psyche, it is no surprise that the flipped classroom can come as a shock to parents. Watching videos on YouTube? That isn't homework! If the kids are doing homework in class, then class must be a glorified study hall. It's a cop-out for lazy teachers! You aren't teaching if you aren't lecturing! The students aren't all looking toward the front of the class; in fact, they're all doing different things! They must not be paying attention. The class is noisy, messy, chaotic. I want my child out of this class!!

PREPARING PARENTS FOR FLIPPING

It is the wise teacher who prepares not just her students, but also their parents, for flipping. As they demystify flipping, teachers can get parents on their side early.

Colleen Kennedy, a teacher at Robbinsdale Armstrong High School in Plymouth, Minnesota, describes an eye-opening encounter she had with a parent. Kennedy was sending home lessons on video two or three times a week as the homework preparation for her precalculus class. A few weeks into the school year, a parent and her son came together to a parent–teacher conference. The parent complained that her son wasn't doing well in the class and asked why. Kennedy asked, "Is he watching the videos?" The parent replied, "Videos? What videos? Hey, wait a minute. . ."

The parent and her son stepped out into the hall and had a lively discussion. After a few moments they returned and, according to Kennedy, "The parent let me know that from now on I would be seeing a marked improvement in her son's math work!"

Kennedy began to e-mail parents when her students were having problems, and asked if they wanted to be on the list to receive reminders that videos were going home. It became an important way to ensure that parents could work with their children as they watched the video lessons (C. Kennedy, personal communication, June 18, 2013).

Communicate Every Way Possible

Kennedy's experience is not that unusual. Flipping teachers are learning it's important to communicate with all parents, not just those whose students are struggling. Byron math teacher Jennifer Green agrees. When she began flipping her math classes, a parent set her this email:

> I'm a bit uncomfortable with the teaching method for this geometry class in that there is no textbook to use as a reference. As far as I can tell, my son takes notes in class and then completes the worksheets as homework. The only reference is the online homework answers. If his notes are not complete, he has no other option but to look at the homework answers. (Green & Fulton, 2013)

After Ms. Green called the parent and explained how she was teaching via the flipped classroom, the parent sent her another email:

> Holy cow! I had no idea all of those options are available! I can now do a better job of planning methods of early,

subtle intervention prior to tests. Thank you! (Green & Fulton, 2013)

Teachers like Green recognize that it's important that everyone understands how flipping the classroom will affect the parents and their children. The message should be upbeat, as was this from Green to parents:

Good news: Your child will never have to miss a class, even if she has to be at swim team finals for three days in a neighboring state. Good news: I will have more time to work with your child. We will cover content in depth. And, best news of all: If your child is having trouble with his homework, I will be there to help—you don't have to struggle to provide that help at home! (Green & Fulton, 2013)

Clintondale High School Principal Greg Green puts it this way:

Was there parental resistance at first? Some had to get their heads around the idea, but when we asked them "How many times were you not able to help your kid with homework?" they saw the value. Many of our parents came up in a different era—back then they could get through school without taking major exams. But when their kids have trouble preparing for high stakes testing, they don't have to be able to help fill in the gaps. Now they know that the expert is right here in school—the teacher can help the students—as it should be! I don't get nearly as many voicemail messages from parents now; they can see we are working with their kids! (Mull, 2011)

When asked how best to communicate with parents, high school physics teacher Kathryn Lanier says,

We use every kind of information possible: posting on our websites, videos, notes home, letters, flyers, parent night, "call me" notes we send home with students, you name it.

And I have different messages on my website at the beginning of the year, throughout the year, and at the end of the year. (Lanier, 2013)

Communicating with parents early can diffuse potential problems. For example, teachers often find it useful to send surveys home to parents before school begins to find out what kind of technology is available for the student to use. April Burton, a French teacher at Francis Howell Central High School in St. Charles, Missouri, created the survey in Figure 7.1. She sent the information home with course materials at the beginning of the school year and also posted it on her class website for parents to complete. The majority of her students' parents completed it, providing her valuable information about technology availability in their homes and, importantly, the parents' views about technology uses in the classroom.

If a family's technology resources are limited, collecting information like this ahead of time makes it easier for teachers to create work-arounds before the child is stigmatized or held back by not having what's needed to watch the lessons. Parents appreciate it when teachers make the extra effort to be sure their children have access, by putting lessons on flash drives or DVDs, arranging for students to borrow school laptops or tablets to take home, or working with them before or after school to watch lessons in the classroom, library, or technology center. Teachers can work with parents to find the solution that works best for each family.

Pointers for Parents

There are many ways teachers can encourage parents to help their children adapt to the flipped classroom. Videos sent home to parents are one effective tool. Although there are many videos about flipped classrooms on the Internet, most parents like to see their child's teacher explaining exactly what to expect in his or her classroom. For example, middle school math teacher Cathelyne Joseph developed a short,

Figure 7.1 Technology Parent Survey

Thank you so much for taking the time to complete this survey. Technology is an ever-growing field, and an area that often catches our students' interests. I love to use technology in the classroom, but I would like a better understanding of where parents stand on this issue. Please understand that the results of this survey will not be shared with the students. It is solely for the purpose of helping me to understand how technology is used at home.

Required

Do you have high-speed Internet access in your home?*

❑ Yes
❑ No

Do you currently have a copy of Microsoft Word or Open Office Writer installed on your home computer?

❑ Yes
❑ No
❑ Other application with the ability to edit Microsoft Word documents

Does your computer have an installed and working printer?

❑ Yes
❑ No

Do you mind downloading and installing free programs such as Microsoft Photo Story, Open Office, Acrobat Reader, Quicktime, etc., for educational purposes?* Step-by-step instructions for download and installation would be provided.

❑ Yes
❑ No

Have you purchased a USB flash drive or other storage media for your child to use for school?

❑ Yes
❑ No
❑ He/she can borrow one of ours if necessary.

Would you allow your son/daughter to have a Gmail account?*

❑ Yes
❑ No
❑ He/She already has one.

Does your son/daughter have a cell phone with unlimited texting?

❏ Yes
❏ No
❏ Not unlimited texting, but he/she could text for educational purposes.

Does your child have a device (i.e., iPod Touch, iPad, tablet) which he/she can use at school to connect to the school's wifi?

❏ Yes
❏ No
❏ I am not sure.

Does your son/daughter have a phone that can access the Internet?

❏ Yes
❏ No
❏ Yes, but he/she is not allowed to use this feature.

How often does your son/daughter use the Internet to study?

❏ Never
❏ Rarely
❏ From time to time
❏ Often
❏ That is the only way he/she studies.

Have you ever purchased a device app or computer software to help your child with school? An app would typically be installed on an Apple, Android, Microsoft, or Blackberry device.

❏ Yes
❏ No
❏ I have never done so, but would be willing to.

What are your thoughts about the use of technology in the classroom?

_____

_____

_____

_____

What is your child's name? _____

Source: Burton (2012)

engaging cartoon with music that introduces students and parents to what her flipped classroom will be like (Joseph, 2012). Videos like these give parents helpful hints for ensuring their children use the homework videos successfully. Pointers include suggestions that parents make sure their children have dedicated time, a stable Internet connection, and a quiet space (with no distractions!) for watching the lesson videos at home. If technology isn't available at home, parents are encouraged to make allowances for the child to stay after school or go in early to watch the videos on school or library computers. Parent videos also encourage them to remind students to pause and rewind the videos as often as needed to be sure they understand the information. And, just as they keep track of other homework assignments, parents should check the notes students take on the videos. Parents are often invited to watch the videos along with their children, so they can provide assistance tailored to the way the teacher is presenting material—and provide feedback to teachers about how well their child is adapting to the flipped classroom.

High school parents are just as likely to be concerned about flipping as parents of younger children. Canadian math teacher Graham Johnson originally made a 15-minute video for the parents of his students to watch, but soon realized that even 15 minutes was too long for busy parents. He shortened it and adapted it to make it interactive, allowing parents to click on the questions they might have, so they could get to the heart of their concerns and share their questions directly with Johnson.

Letting Parents Experience a Flipped Classroom

Teachers who are flipping often use Back to School Night to demonstrate what occurs in their classes. Because these are usually held in the first few weeks of school, around the time teachers have introduced the concept to their students and are ready to begin flipping, the timing is good. Some creative teachers have even flipped Back to School Night! Here's the approach taken by two Virginia social studies teachers, Frank Franz and Ken Halla:

> Frank is flipping his back to school night (in VA we have the parents come in and meet the teachers for 10 minutes). So Frank (and I this year) are e-mailing our parents our flipped video and then giving them a Google form for their questions. Then, for the 10 minutes we see them (we) will go over the questions and additional ones that come up so the parents can actually experience what their kids are doing in class. (Halla, 2013)

This hands-on approach can make all the difference in calming the fears of concerned parents.

Reaching All Caregivers

Communications about flipping are especially important for reaching parents who might not come to school events like Back to School Night. Some have work schedules making it difficult to come to school; others have language barriers or negative associations with their own schooling experiences that make them uncomfortable visiting their children's classrooms.

Thoughtful teachers have developed helpful strategies to convey to these parents what is happening in their classrooms. One prekindergarten teacher records videos of herself reading to small groups of students. She sends these videos home for students and parents to watch together. For those parents who don't speak English, watching the videos with their children can be a great way to help the parents with their own English skills. (It's also a great way to figure out how to pronounce all those made-up words in the Dr. Seuss books their children adore!)

Grandparents and other caregivers are also tuning in to the lesson videos. Byron's Jennifer Green tells the story of one of her students who was really struggling in school, a potential dropout in his sophomore year. His grandfather took it upon himself to help. But it was a long time since the grandfather had taken geometry, and he was not sure of the content and didn't want to make things worse by confusing the young man.

The grandfather started watching Ms. Green's math videos with his grandson. He was excited to be able to rekindle his own memory of geometry, and to begin to appreciate the new ways that geometry was being taught in Ms. Green's class. A few weeks into the semester the grandfather sent the following message to Ms. Green:

> Over the last three weeks I have seen a noticeable improvement in his comprehension of the material. I realize that I have only studied with him through Unit 4 and now starting Unit 5 but am curious whether you have seen any improvement in his quiz and test scores? I am still very impressed with the Moodle site and only wish these resources had been available when I worked with my other grandchildren and even my daughter! Great site, keep up the good work! (Green & Fulton, 2013)

The young man ended up doing just fine in geometry and graduated from high school, with his grandfather in the audience, cheering him on with pride!

CAVEATS

Flipping the classroom also means flipping the time spent at home. It requires shifts for parents as well as students. If a student has video assignments in two, three, or four classes a night—and other students in a family are also assigned work that also requires time on the computer—scheduling and sharing one or a limited number of devices can be a nightmare. And parents also often need time on the computer when they get home from work. As one parent said, "Each of my kids gets one hour of computer time for homework in the evening after supper. With one computer and three kids, that means it's often after 11 p.m. when I get to go on the computer—and then I have to fight over that time with my husband!"

Parents rightly complain that the pressure to purchase more machines and more high–speed, high-capacity data plans for each of their kids' smartphones is putting a major strain on their finances. How can you say no when they say they need it for schoolwork?

Furthermore, while videos sent home can help parents gain a window into their children's classrooms, this may not be the case for parents who don't speak English. In schools where 10, 15, or even 20 or more languages are spoken at home, teachers are challenged to find ways to keep the communications open to all parents, so they too are aware of the teaching their children are receiving.

Last, although teachers typically value more parental involvement, which may increase as parents watch lessons sent home with students, can too much involvement become a problem? Are teachers finding that parents are second-guessing the teacher's instructional methods or content as they watch lesson videos with their kids? Might teachers' burdens be increased by parents commenting in classroom chats or e-mailing them about their children's lessons?

One flipping math teacher found herself slightly intimidated when a top-notch mathematician, the parent of one of her students, informed her, "I've been watching all the videos to be sure you are teaching well." Fortunately, the parent concluded that he was indeed pleased with her teaching!

SUMMARY

- Flipping can seem strange to parents; it's a far cry from what they experienced in school.

- Parental support for flipping is important. Teachers are reaching out to parents in a variety of ways to ensure they are comfortable with the new instructional approach their children are experiencing and can support their children appropriately.

- Flipping Back to School Night and sending videos home to parents are two approaches teachers have found useful.

- Once they know what to expect and how to help their children become successful with flipped learning, parents are usually enthusiastic about being able to see what their children are learning. They can be reassured that they don't have to be the content experts when their children struggle with homework.

- Adjustments to home life come with flipped classrooms. Sharing time on a limited number of computers or devices, purchasing more devices, and making upgrades to existing systems are concerns to parents.

- Teachers may have to adjust to the fact that, by providing windows into their teaching via videos, greater parental engagement may be translated as more parental input, critiques, and commentaries on their teaching.

8

Flipping Makes Effective Use of Resources

Flipping With Districtwide Technology Access

Matt Akin, Superintendent, Piedmont City Schools, Piedmont, Alabama

Piedmont City Schools superintendent Matt Akin sees technology as a way to level the playing field in his small rural district (three schools) where 68% of his 1,200 students are eligible for free and reduced-price lunch. He's been creative in finding ways to ensure that all students have equal access to the resources necessary to learn. For example, in 2010, Piedmont was selected as one of 20 school districts across the nation for the E-rate pilot program

"Learning on the Go." Through this project, Piedmont was able to build a network that created a "wireless cloud" over the entire city, providing free Internet access for all families. When implementation of the grant ended in March 2013, the city and district agreed to split the cost (approximately $50 per year per household) of leasing access to the network, so all households continue to have free Internet access.

The district also undertook a one-to-one laptop initiative that provides a MacBook Air laptop computer for every student in grades 4–12 to take home. Students in grades 1–3 have one-to-one access to laptops, tablets, and iPads for use in the classroom. Akin estimates the district spends approximately 5% of its $10 million annual budget on hardware, software, and digital content, including subscriptions to a learning management system for all teachers.

Flipping the classroom is a normal part of instructional practice now that technology provides true "anywhere, anytime" learning, according to Akin. Most of his teachers, across all grade levels and subjects, flip at least some of their classes. "The eighth-grade Algebra I teacher probably flips her class every day, and, on any given night you'll see fourth- and fifth-grade lessons being sent home for students to watch," according to Akin. He cites a visit he made to a fourth-grade classroom where one student, working on double-digit division problems, was explaining her solutions to other students who were still working on single-digit problems. They'd all watched a Khan Academy video the previous night and were working at their own pace on increasingly difficult problems.

Akin notes another benefit: Many of the students are "pretty transient," even within the community:

> I'll drive kids home from football practice and some nights they may be going home, other nights I drop them at Grandma's because both parents are working. But because we have a wireless cloud over the city, teachers know the kids can connect and do their lessons wherever they are.

He also believes that flipping is of special help to students who may not have a lot of parental support at home to help them with traditional homework:

This makes it possible to extend the learning environment for them. Kids can move at their own pace, in the comfort and safety of own environment, watching a lesson over and over if need be, and then take the quizzes on the LMS to check their mastery. The next day, the teacher knows who needs extra help, without the embarrassment to kids of having to raise their hands in class when they don't get it.

Akin is optimistic that flipped teaching will be an important resource for teaching to the Common Core standards. With class time freed up by sending lessons home, teachers will have more opportunities to individualize instruction and help students build deeper understanding of the material.

Source: M. Akin (personal communication, November 7, 2013)

The Piedmont story shows how flipping can be viewed as a natural byproduct of investments districts are making to support technology initiatives. And indeed, one of the most compelling arguments in support of flipping is the digital conversion taking place in today's schools. With e-books and e-learning, texting and twittering, Google and GPS devices, technology is no longer "nice to have" in today's schools; it is an essential part of everyday teaching and learning. As schools continue to invest in these resources, more schools have the technological readiness that makes flipping the classroom far more possible than would have been the case just a few short years ago.

THE PUSH/PULL OF TECHNOLOGY INNOVATION AND IMPLEMENTATION

The move toward flipping may be an outgrowth of the push/pull theory of technology implementation. It's a symbiotic, cyclical pattern: Ever more powerful, flexible, user-friendly and affordable technologies create a "technology push" that drives usage; at the same time, the "market pull" side of the equation—teachers, administrators, and even parents and students—create a demand driving the development of new tools and applications. This framework suggests that new technologies that are powerful and easy to use, matched with a growing base of ready and willing users, make flipped teaching part of a natural evolution of teaching with technology.

TECHNOLOGY ADOPTION IN K–12 EDUCATION

We've come a long way since the early days of computers in schools. Twenty-five years ago, in a report to Congress on the potential of technology for education, analysts reported that 95% of public *schools* had *at least one* computer for instructional use (U.S. Congress, 1988). Today there is hardly a classroom to be found without some technology in it. In 2009, virtually all (97%) of *teachers* had one or more computers for instruction in their classrooms (National Center of Education Statistics [NCES], 2009). The student-to-computer ratio, once measured as hundreds of students per computer, has hovered around a little over a 3:1 ratio for several years. However, that ratio does not count tablets and other devices that are now the building blocks of many one-to-one technology initiatives in schools (Fletcher, Schaffhauser, & Levin, 2012). Clearly, there's a lot of technology in classrooms today.

Internet in K–12 schools reveals even more dramatic growth. Some of us remember the first Net Day in 1996, climbing on ladders and pulling fiber through ceiling tiles in our neighborhood schools in support of the Clinton administration's effort to wire all the nation's K–12 schools. Congress had just passed the Telecommunications Act of 1996, which authorized the E-rate program to ensure access to affordable telecommunications service. It's made a huge difference. At that time, only 14% of schools and libraries had access to the Internet, and it was mainly dial-up service. Less than 10 years later, in 2005, almost all schools and 94% of all instructional classrooms had Internet access (Federal Communications Commission, 2013). Most recently, the FCC announced in February 2014 that the government plans to double the funds available through the E-rate program, adding $1 billion a year to ensure that all schools and libraries have broadband access to the Internet (at speeds of 100 Mbps or higher) (Fung, 2013).

In the early days, school administrators had a simple shopping list: computers and wires. Today they are faced with long lists of hardware, software, tools, platforms, and systems needed to support a range of educational needs and opportunities. Workstations and laptop computers, tablets and e-readers, interactive whiteboards and LCD projectors, smartphones, digital cameras, learning management systems, computer-based testing systems—the list goes on and on. Not to mention the current holy grail: wireless access throughout the school.

Current data indicate that 59% of teachers have interactive whiteboards in the classroom (up from 23% in 2009), and over a third have handhelds (36%, including cell phones and smartphones) and tablets or electronic readers (35%) available in their classrooms (NCES, 2009; PBS, 2013). The growth of tablets and e-readers is particularly dynamic: In 2012, one in five teachers reported they used a tablet or e-reader in their classrooms; a year later, over a third of teachers said they were using these tools in teaching (PBS, 2013).

DIGITAL READINESS

In the old days, one of the biggest concerns was providing teachers a vision of why and how they would use technology. Today most teachers don't have to be convinced of the value of technology for teaching. When asked what they believe are the benefits of educational technology, three quarters of teachers in a recent national online survey said they believe it can reinforce and expand content and motivate students to learn (PBS, 2013). Most also believe technology can help respond to a variety of learning styles (73%), make it possible for them to "do much more than ever before for my students" (69%), and "demonstrate something I can't show in any other way" (65%) (PBS, 2013).

Administrators share these views. Seventy-four percent of administrators responding to the 2011 Speak Up survey said they believe digital content increases student engagement, and 50% said it helps to personalize instruction (Project Tomorrow, 2012a). In fact, once considered dinosaurs in terms of technological uptake, today's administrators are more likely to be technology users than the general public. According to this same survey, in 2011, when less than half of all Americans (46%) were smartphone users, almost three-quarters (71%) of district administrators had already started using smartphones. More than half (55%) used tablets, as compared to just 10% of the rest of America (Project Tomorrow, 2012b). Once a superintendent or principal starts to use technological tools for personal use, he or she is more likely to appreciate the power of these tools for educational productivity and champion their use in schools.

BUT THE MORE WE HAVE, THE MORE WE WANT

Despite this rapid adoption, teachers and administrators aren't satisfied with what they have. More than two thirds of teachers—and three quarters of those who teach in low-income schools—say they need more classroom technology (PBS, 2013). Only 15% of district administrators and technology leaders say they have enough bandwidth to meet current needs, and 71% of district technology leaders say they cannot ensure their teachers they can meet future needs for classroom connectivity (Project Tomorrow, 2013b).

Although districts are struggling to provide wireless connectivity to their schools and classrooms, until this occurs, the potential of anywhere, anytime computing in schools is limited. Furthermore, as discussed earlier, tech-savvy students and their parents are not satisfied with the status quo; the demand for more use of technology in schools is a hunger that must continually be fed.

WHERE'S THE MONEY TO PAY FOR ALL THIS?

Technology remains a huge investment as schools struggle to upgrade what they have and stay current with new technologies. With learning management systems that help teachers keep tabs on student progress, smartboards and software, annual subscriptions to Internet service providers, conversions to wireless, and a host of other must-have technology resources for education, the bills just keep rising.

Although school budgets have always been tight, funding cutbacks over the last few years have hit technology budgets particularly hard. In the Speak Up survey for 2012, three quarters (74%) of administrators reported that they had less money for technology than they did five years earlier (Project Tomorrow, 2013b). For some, it meant maintaining the status quo (48%) on instructional technology projects or postponing new projects (37%), but for others it meant cutting back on existing activities to save money (32%). According to Doug Levin, Director of the State Educational Technology Directors Association, only a third of schools have money budgeted separately for technology (Bui, 2013).

In addition, teacher training and support are continuing costs that don't go away, even if teachers are taking on more self-training and learning from peers on their professional networks. Furthermore, when teachers put in extra hours to create videos, monitor student work, and make themselves available to students and parents online at all hours of the day, their time is a cost that must be factored, even if it is calculated as an opportunity cost that keeps them from family and personal pursuits. Those lost hours can lead to teacher burnout, a factor in the loss of good but exhausted teachers if they feel unappreciated for their innovative efforts.

Making Budgets Stretch Further: Switching to Digital Content

According to the State Education Technology Directors Association (SETDA), states and districts spend $5.5 billion a year in core instructional content, but much of that is for textbooks with content that is 7 to 10 years old (Fletcher, Schaffhauser, & Levin, 2012). However, that is changing rapidly. In 2011 digital textbooks were estimated to represent just 3% of the education textbook market. According to the SETDA report, as of 2012, 22 states had changed their definition of textbooks, allowed funding flexibility that permits using textbook funds to support digital content (changing "book dollars into device dollars," allowing for the purchase of devices on which digital content can be accessed), or launched their own digital textbook or Open Educational Resources initiatives.

Because of these policy changes at the state and district levels, many expect the switch to digital educational resources to come quickly. One textbook distribution company estimates that by 2014, the digital textbook adoption rate will be 19.5% and that it will reach 50% by 2018 (Reynolds, 2012).

The move to digital textbooks makes dollars and sense. As the SEDTA report notes, a traditional print textbook can cost up to or over $100 per student. These are valuable resources that must be used year after year, often amortized over six or more years as part of a district's strict textbook adoption cycle. Students don't have a sense of ownership for them when they aren't allowed to write in them or even, in some cases, take them home! In contrast, digital content is flexible, can be assembled in a variety of ways in a variety of formats, and is increasingly created, shared, and "owned" by teachers and students themselves.

The term *textbook* is becoming almost obsolete, as curricula are being supported by a range of apps, cloud-computing resources, shareware, and other free and low-cost content resources. And it's not just textbook dollars that are being freed up by the switch to digital content. Around the nation, schools are reviewing all aspects of their budgets—including technology budgets—to find savings. For example, when one school gave every student a laptop, they realized they no longer needed student response systems (clickers) in every classroom (Levin, 2011); instead, teachers capture screen shots from each student's laptop in real time to see how many students (and which ones) got the correct answer.

In the Byron school district, not having money for new textbooks ultimately led to the flipped classroom model. When the math teachers created their own curricula, using online resources and their own videos, the principal estimated they freed up $40,000 to $60,000 in textbook savings ($90 per student) in just the first year. He used this savings to hire another staff person (M. Duffy, personal communication, October 3, 2011).

Saving Money With BYOD Policies

If I had to buy 700 smartphones for the students at our school, where almost all of our students are eligible for free and reduced price lunch, it would be impossible. But even the poorest students have acquired their own devices in the last few years, so I was able to put our money into investing in a robust learning management system. All my teachers can use this to support their teaching, and it has been a real boon for those teachers who are flipping their instruction. (D. Pinder, personal communication, May 28, 2013)

Another approach is perhaps the most far-reaching in terms of educational impact: Administrators are dropping their previous reluctance to allow students to bring their own devices into the classroom. The BYOD (bring your own device) movement may be the hottest new trend in educational technology. It certainly is a factor in flipped learning.

As discussed in Chapter 6, students' personal access to mobile technologies is growing rapidly. In the fall of 2011, 26% of students in grades 6–8 said that they had personal access (not school provided) to a tablet computer (Project Tomorrow,

2013c). By 2013, this percentage had jumped to 60%. Almost three quarters of middle schoolers surveyed had personal access to a smartphone (73%), as did 9 out of 10 of their high school peers (89%), half of students in grades 3–5, and even 22% of students in grades K–2! (Evans, 2014).

In 2011, half of the district administrators surveyed did not allow students to use their personal mobile devices in school, but just one year later, that figure dropped to just over a third (35%) banning personal devices. Not surprisingly, it is administrators who are mobile technology users themselves who lead the BYOD bandwagon: 41% of district administrators who currently use a smartphone or tablet were evaluating a BYOD policy, and 15% were piloting such an approach. Principals too are dropping their bans on use of personal devices, with 36% of those surveyed saying they expect to put a BYOD policy in place (Project Tomorrow, 2013b). In fact, that estimate was low; recent data indicate that 56% of districts have adopted BYOD policies, with 84% of high schools and 74% of middle schools allowing students to use personal mobile devices in school (Schaffhauser, 2014).

A combination of BYOD and converting to digital content made it possible for principal Greg Green to implement flipped classrooms at his high-need, low-income high school:

> We aren't a wealthy district by any stretch of the imagination, but most of our kids can access YouTube, and most have cell phones. We use the classroom resources; send things home however they need it, and some watch at the beginning of class. (G. Green, personal communication, May 21, 2013)

He's pleased with how the switch to flipping has saved the district money:

> Clintondale is not anywhere near a 1:1 environment. But the kids have the devices—especially smartphones—so it's not a case of having to buy technology for every student. Eighty-two percent of our students use their own devices to watch the videos. (G. Green, personal communication, May 21, 2013)

Green notes how the district has accommodated itself to students' using their personal devices in school.

> In general, our school's policy is "Don't punish the device, punish the behavior." It's not the device that's a problem, it's the inappropriate usage. Teachers can control the environment—if they want to have cell phones in class or not, it's their call. But we don't even think of them as phones—they have so many other uses. (G. Green, personal communication, May 21, 2013)

When he saw how well his students were responding to flipped lessons created by his teachers, he saw the value of dropping the 1:1 textbook model they'd always used.

> Instead of spending $10,000–$15,000 to buy a textbook for every student, I can buy just a few for each classroom, making it possible for teachers to have multiple texts to draw on for their teaching. And I can use the rest of the money to buy other resources for the classroom, including technological tools. (G. Green, personal communication, May 21, 2013)

CAVEATS

Despite the continuing and strong growth of technologies in schools, the digital divide is still a concern. While the divide may be narrowing, with more schools adopting 1:1 technology initiatives, the BYOD movement is not without equity issues. To adopt BYOD programs, the State of Texas implemented a $10 million technology lending program to cover students who do not have their own devices (Fletcher, Schaffhauser, & Levin, 2012). Furthermore, there continue to be concerns about students whose access to content is limited by the speed of their connections, the power of their personal devices, and the data plans they can afford when compared to those of their more affluent peers.

One of the biggest concerns regarding the digital divide is not access per se, but how technology is used to support learning. A recent analysis of the 2009 and 2011 NAEP data found that more than half of black students taking the math exams reported they used computers for math drills in school, while less than a third (30%) of white students said they used computers for drills. Looking at comparisons by income groups, the data were similar: 41% of low-income students reported using computers for drill work vs. 29% of students who were above the free and reduced-price lunch income line (Reich, 2013).

Will this trend—teaching practices that consign low-income and minority students to less creative uses of technology—continue in flipped classrooms? The study reminds us of how important it is to dig deeper and look beyond mere numbers, analyzing how students use technologies to advance their learning in all classrooms.

States and districts will continue to need to address a number of policy issues to facilitate digital conversions and cost-effective use of resources that support flipped classrooms. These include teacher training and support, changes in school culture and practices, quality control, intellectual property and reuse rights, and assurances that sustainable funding is available for updating necessary devices, content, and robust Internet connectivity.

SUMMARY

- The push/pull of technology innovation and implementation means that past and present technology investments, along with teacher, student, and administrator readiness, have made the adoption of flipped classroom approaches much more feasible today than would have been possible in the past.

- Nevertheless, stretched and limited school budgets are forcing educators to look at innovative ways to provide educational services to all students. Among these measures are the switch to digital content and adoption of Bring Your Own Device (BYOD) initiatives.

- Despite this progress with technology, the digital divide remains a concern. This is related both to students' varying access to devices as well as the need to pay attention to the differing ways these devices are used to support learning.

- States and districts will need to review their policies and keep ahead of challenges (i.e., funding, broadband, training, school culture, quality control, and intellectual property) that could impede or block further effective adoptions of flipped classrooms.

9

Flipping Builds 21st Century Skills

"Hey Dude, Here's the Answer!"

A teacher assigns a problem for her physics class: Find the kinetic energy of 5,400 cubic meters of helium at a temperature of 283 degrees Kelvin. One student goes deep into his textbook, paws through his class notes, desperately trying to recall the lesson that covered this topic, but he is stumped. His buddy Googles "Calculating Kinetic Energy," and up pops http://www.dummies.com/how-to/content/calculating-kinetic-energy-in-an-ideal-gas.html. He plugs in the numbers, then turns to his friend and says, "Hey dude, here's the answer!"

Source: Bergmann & Sams (2013b).

Navigating to find information today is more than just knowing how to Google a question to find an instant answer; it's changed the way we think about information. It wasn't so long ago that arguments around the dinner table were solved when Dad reached for the *Encyclopedia Britannica* and had his son look up "kinetic energy." While today's technique for finding information is faster, not everyone is comfortable with what this means for education. If the facts are all out there, accessible at an instant's mouse click or finger jab, who needs to memorize them?

Clearly, it's important to know that "in 1492 Columbus sailed the ocean blue," but it's more important to know why he went and what happened afterward. The reality of the Google Generation is that, with information compounding at geometric rates every day, and with smart tools in our hands to find it, the skills students need to be thoughtful, informed, and productive in the information age are different. These are indeed 21st century skills.

FIRST CENTURY SKILLS IS MORE LIKE IT

It wasn't so long ago that the phrase "the turn of the century" meant moving from the 1800s into the 1900s, signaling the dawn of the 20th century. It was a time of major change in the economic, social, and political realities all across the globe. Even back then, John Dewey noted that schools were changing curriculum and teaching methods based on the new demands of commerce, business, and technology (as it was defined then) (Dewey, 2001 [1915]).

But that was nothing compared to the excitement heralded by moving from the 20th century into the new millennium. With the forces of globalization and technology came a whole new way of thinking about education, with educators around the globe debating, and eventually defining, the 21st century skills all students need to be successful for life and work. Some have suggested we call these "first century skills" to denote the new world represented by this first century in the new millennium. Characterizing students born after the turn of the new millennium as *neomillennials*, educators have also defined "neomillennial learning styles" that learners bring with them to today's educational settings (Dede, 2010).

Nonetheless, *21st century skills* is the label that has stuck. These typically build on a framework developed by education, business, and government leaders that go beyond the 3 Rs to include world languages, arts, economics, science, geography, history, and government and civics (Partnership for 21st Century Skills, n.d.). Woven throughout these core subjects are critical themes that include global awareness; financial, economic, business, and entrepreneurial literacy; and civic, health, and environmental literacies. These are each further broken down into subsets of

- Learning and innovation skills (often defined as the 4 C's: creativity, critical thinking, communication, and collaboration);
- Information, media, and technology skills; and
- Life and career skills (flexibility and adaptability, initiative and self-direction, social and cross-cultural skills, productivity and accountability, and leadership and responsibility).

Other organizations have created similar frameworks that define 21st century skills in similar ways, with slight variations, emphases, and subsets. Currently, a high-level group of business, government, and academic partners known as ATC21S (Assessment and Teaching of 21st Century Skills, atc21s.org) are engaging more than 250 researchers across 60 institutions worldwide to provide an updated, internationally agreed-upon framework for 21st century skills. ATC21S has categorized 21st century skills into four broad categories:

- **Ways of thinking.** Creativity, critical thinking, problem-solving, decision-making and learning
- **Ways of working.** Communication and collaboration
- **Tools for working.** Information and communications technology (ICT) and information literacy
- **Skills for living in the world.** Citizenship, life and career, and personal and social responsibility (ATC21S, n.d.)

This international group is currently is focusing on two skill areas that span these four categories.

- **Collaborative problem-solving.** Working together to solve a common challenge, which involves the contribution and exchange of ideas, knowledge or resources to achieve the goal; and
- **ICT literacy—learning in digital networks.** Learning through digital means, such as social networking, ICT literacy, technological awareness and simulation. (ATC21S, n.d.)

The group's focus on these skill areas is based on their belief that each of these elements is important to ensure individuals can function in social networks and contribute to the development of social and intellectual capital.

In all these endeavors, the goal has always been to help educators embed these skills throughout their normal coursework. Early on, there was some pushback from some teachers—is this one more thing I have to teach in a crowded curriculum? But as the technology continues to advance and the world shrinks, teachers recognize that there is an ever-growing demand that they help their students develop the skills and competencies necessary to ensure success in today's global information economy.

The graphic in Figure 9.1 illustrates one educator's take on 21st century skills for students.

WORKFORCE SUCCESS AND SCHOOL SKILLS

A 2013 study conducted by the Gallup organization confirms that we still have a long way to go in ensuring that these skills are part of the learning of all students (Microsoft Partners in Learning, The Pearson Foundation, & Gallup, 2013). In this survey, a random sample of 1,014 young adults were asked about the correlations between the skills they use in the workforce, their success, and whether 21st century skills (defined as collaboration, skilled communication, knowledge construction,

Figure 9.1   Students' Skills in the 21st Century Education

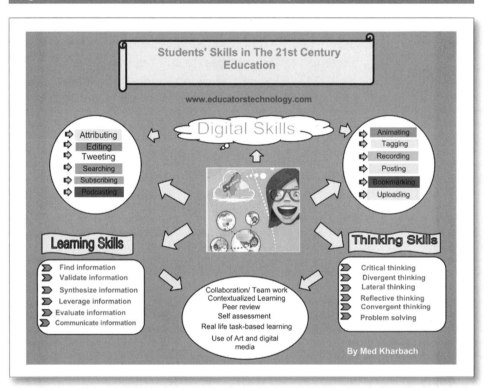

Source: Kharbach (n.d.), http://www.educatorstechnology.com/2013/11/25-important-skills-for-21st-century.html.

global awareness, technology for learning, self-regulation, and real-world problem solving) were a part of their education in their last year of schooling (high school, undergraduate, or graduate school).

Among the findings were the following:

- The majority (59%) reported that most of the skills they use in their current job were developed outside of school.
- Among all the 21st century skills, real-world problem solving was the most highly ranked driver of high work quality. Less than two thirds of those surveyed (63%) reported developing this skill "often" in the last year of school; for high school graduates, only 39% reported this skill was developed in their last year of school.

- Those who reported high 21st century skill development were twice as likely to have high work quality as compared to those with low 21st century skill development.
- Although most (86%) reported using computers or technology to complete assignments during their last year in school, only 14% reported working often with others using video conference or online collaboration tools in school.
- Younger respondents (aged 18–22) reported slightly higher levels of 21st century skill development, which study authors suggest may indicate a change in teaching strategies.
- Those who had not graduated from high school or who had only a high school degree reported lower levels of 21st century skill development than did respondents with college and graduate educations.

WHERE DOES FLIPPING FIT IN?

Collaborative Problem Solving in a Flipped French Classroom

April Burton, Francis Howell Central High School, St. Charles, Missouri

One of my favorite things about conducting a flipped classroom is that it allows for the inclusion of so many cooperative learning activities. I love watching as students take the teacher role and teach each other. However, cooperative learning has its challenges. How does a teacher ensure that each student benefits from the cooperative learning activity? How does one avoid having "bogs"—students who do all the work—and "logs"—students who just sit there and take up space? In small groups I give jobs to each person so that each person is responsible for something and those jobs switch throughout the activity.

Today, I used cooperative learning with large groups and with an application to the real world. This activity was a lot of fun. It got crazy, but that is normal for my classroom. For this activity, I told students that we would be part of a "corporation." I am the CEO; I give the paycheck (aka: grade). They would be working in committees. Each committee was assigned a category of regular verbs. They would be responsible for teaching (or really reviewing because this is level 2) the conjugations, providing a clever way of remembering how to conjugate these verbs, and providing a list of common verbs in the category, as well as what those verbs are in English. To make this activity work like it would in a business place, each committee had to choose a foreman (or "patron"). I, as the CEO, would communicate with this foreman. Within each committee, they had to divide into sub-committees. One would be in charge of creating an engaging presentation; the other was in charge of creating an activity which would allow the rest of the class to participate in practicing the grammar point. Students had 40 minutes to work. I called a "board meeting" 15 minutes after they had started working to touch base with the foremen and to make sure that each group was on track . . . I asked them about their method of presentation, as well as the type of activity that their group would be doing. I talked to them about their committee members who were being "logs" and gave them ideas of how they could get those team members involved.

It was a great experience. The students amazed me with their enthusiasm. It was fun to watch the foremen as they moved within their groups to delegate jobs. I loved hearing the conversations about what types of practice activities would be the most beneficial for their classmates. As any CEO would do, I guided them when necessary and encouraged good behaviors. Tomorrow the groups will present. We'll see how those presentations go.

Source: Burton (2013)

Educators like April Burton, an ardent proponent of flipped teaching, are enthusiastic in their views that the flipped classroom supports an almost seamless embedding of 21st century skills in their daily classroom activities. As the example above illustrates, even a class like French can offer opportunities for creative teachers to focus on collaboration, cooperation, and communication skills—especially when the content delivery via homework lessons frees up classroom time for practice and creative activities like the one described above.

When teachers are no longer expected to serve as the only source of wisdom, they can encourage students to find information on their own—a major first century skill. The critical role for a teacher is guidance: helping students to think carefully about the sources they have chosen and to distinguish which information sources are accurate, most appropriate, or best suited to their own learning goals and styles. The question is no longer just "What's the answer?" but also "Where did you find it? Do you believe it? How do you know it's right, true, or the best information?"

And using technology appropriately is part of the process. Physics teacher Katie Lanier puts it this way:

Net etiquette, online coursework, problem solving, presenting and discussing are all areas that students need to be proficient in going forward in their work or school. They need to know where to go to find good sources of information and bring many sources together in the process of problem solving. (Lanier, 2013)

SUPPORTING BLOOM WITH TECHNOLOGY

Educator Kathy Schrock has taken Bloom's taxonomy (see Chapter 1) and mapped how learning skills can be supported with everyday apps, with illustrative graphics for iPad, Android, Google, and Web 2.0 users. Figure 9.2 illustrates how iPad apps support Bloom's revised taxonomy.

In this work, students are using technology for a reason—building skills for learning independently, for monitoring their learning, and for sharing their learning. In flipped classrooms, this occurs in both out-of-class assignments and in-class work.

Figure 9.2 iPad Apps to Support Bloom's Revised Taxonomy

Source: Schrock (n.d.), http://www.schrockguide.net/bloomin-apps.html

When students are engaged in inquiry activities, hands-on lab work, project-based activities, independent study, presentations, peer instruction, or other engaging, stimulating, creative classroom work, they are learning and applying the first century skills necessary for success later in life.

CAVEATS

Finding information is not the same as knowing; accessing is not the same as understanding. Case in point: Searching for an answer to the question posed at the beginning of this chapter,

I did a Google search and was directed to the "chemistry for dummies" website. Yet, after reading their explanation twice, I still don't understand kinetic energy!

Students can too easily become dazzled by the quick or the snazzy without going deep enough for lasting knowledge. Some educators are concerned that students' ways of finding information, communicating, and creating information when using technology may involve shortcuts that also shortcut their deep understanding. In a recent survey of Advanced Placement (AP) and National Writing Project (NWP) teachers at the middle and high school levels, the Pew Center for the Internet and American Life found that, in addition to using digital tools to promote better writing, almost all those surveyed also encourage their students to do at least some writing in the good old-fashioned way: by hand. Some teachers did so because students are still required to write by hand on pencil-and-paper standardized tests, including the AP exams. Other teachers said they required some handwritten assignments because they believe that students "do more active thinking, synthesizing, and editing when writing by hand, and writing by hand discourages any temptation to copy and paste others' work" (Purcell, Buchanan, & Friedrich, 2013, p. 6).

The AP and NWP teachers also expressed concerns about student writing in today's digital environment, including these:

- An increasingly ambiguous line between "formal" and "informal" writing and the tendency of some students to use informal language and style in formal writing assignments

- The increasing need to educate students about writing for different audiences using different voices and registers

- The general cultural emphasis on truncated forms of expression, which some feel is hindering students' willingness and ability to write longer texts and to think critically about complicated topics

- Disparate access to and skill with digital tools among their students

Teachers were divided on the impact of digital tools on these trends:

- 68% said digital tools make students more likely to take shortcuts and not put effort into their writing.

- 46% believed these tools make students more likely to write too fast and be careless.

- Yet, while 40% said today's digital technologies make students more likely to use poor spelling and grammar, an almost equal number (38%) had the opposite opinion: They believe digital technologies make students *less* likely to use poor spelling and grammar.

SUMMARY

- Educators have defined 21st century skills as critical for student success in work, civic, and social success.

- Although the categories and characteristics of 21st century skills are widely accepted, they are not always embedded in the curricula and teaching found in many schools today.

- This gap is revealed in surveys of students who report that most of these skills were developed on the job, rather than in school.

- The flipped classroom can provide an opportunity for teachers to incorporate these skills and competencies in their assignments and classroom activities.

- Unless 21st century skills are built on a strong foundation of basic skills, students may shortcut their deeper understanding. Adopting new skills and ways of knowing does not mean throwing out the underlying values and core competencies of a traditional education.

10
Flipping the Future

These are exciting times for education. The Common Core State Standards put a spotlight on content; teacher evaluation designs target teaching quality; charter schools offer educational options; and technologies bring the world to the desktop, the laptop, and now the personal device of learners.

Where does flipping the classroom fit in? Is it an educational version of what Clayton Christenson describes as a "disruptive innovation" in business: a product or service that, in its very simplicity and accessibility, enters a market at the bottom and gradually displaces more complex competitors—as laptops disrupted the market for mainframes and minicomputers and cell phones disrupted the established market of fixed line telephony (Christensen, 2013). Will flipped teaching become the camel's nose under the tent of education, or a Trojan horse that looks terrific but brings negative unanticipated and unintended consequences? Or is it an educational flash in the pan, a fad with little long-term impact, positive or negative?

The teachers and educators profiled in this book would likely weigh in on the promising side of flipped teaching and learning. Their experience is impressive, and their perspective, which forms the core of this book, is powerful. Like most early adopters, they are naturally enthusiastic and positive. Nonetheless, it's also important to gain the perspective of those outside the movement. In looking to the future of flipping, we solicited views of a group of well-respected educational leaders who, while not actively engaged in the flipped classroom movement, have followed reforms and innovations in education over the years and can bring the long view to this discussion. Their views, summarized below, create a lens for looking into the future of flipping.

HOW MIGHT FLIPPED CLASSROOMS IMPACT EDUCATION?

Devon Jensen, who teaches in the Department of Leadership, Technology, and Human Development in the College of Education at Georgia Southern University, suggests that we are in a unique time, during which the use technology as a vehicle for improved pedagogy, linked with an understanding of student learning and needs, makes flipped teaching a vehicle for positive change:

> One of the challenges facing education today is that learning is structured around pedagogical theory that saw education as a non-technological space. This is not the case anymore and there is now a close connection among pedagogy, content, and technology in contemporary classrooms. In this sense, educators using flipped classrooms do not see technology as a mere tool to enhance learning but as the means through which teachers model how students will need to learn in the future.
>
> 21st Century Learning happens when there is an interaction among content, pedagogy, and technological knowledge. Effective teaching exists in a realm where: there is a

representation of concepts using technologies; there are pedagogical techniques that use technology to teach content; technology is used to help students address the learning problems they face; and where [there is] a knowledge of how technologies can be used to develop new understandings of a student's world. This is how flipped classrooms are impacting education. (D. Jensen, personal communication, September 3, 2013)

Adam Bellow, former teacher and founder and CEO of eduClipper, a free visual bookmarking service for teachers, suggests flipping a classroom can have a major impact on education because

spending more class time exploring concepts, debating ideas, and doing tangible work with the teacher facilitating rather than lecturing students on high-level concepts and asking them to do "work" at home makes the classroom a place of exploration and discovery which is the best way to learn a concept or idea. Instead of memorizing facts or struggling with question sets outside of the classroom, students can work together and with their teacher to find answers, and more importantly understand the how and why of what they are intended to be learning. (A. Bellow, personal communication, August 28, 2013)

WHAT MIGHT OTHER BENEFITS BE?

Lisa Schmucki, the founder of edWeb.net, an online community of educators, pointed out the value of teachers' taking ownership of a new approach. She has seen this teacher-to-teacher enthusiasm at work. She reports that the flipped learning community is one of the fastest growing communities on edWeb, and edWeb's free webinars on flipping draw exceptionally high participation. Schmucki attributes the power of flipped teaching to the fact that it is a shared and highly collaborative approach to teaching and learning.

It is a teacher-led innovation that can be implemented very easily in the classroom, at very little cost. Teachers are so excited when they learn from peers, or in a webinar, about a simple way to flip a classroom that they can try the very next day. The ability for a teacher to implement change that quickly, that has such an impact on the learning process, is very empowering for teachers—and fun for them and their students. It's in the teachers' control, the tools are easily accessible, and they can do it for free with very basic equipment. (L. Schmucki, personal communication, October 1, 2013)

Bellow suggests additional benefits:

The students also all get a (hopefully) high level of quality in the resources that are shared and the idea is that the resources are also all the same for their peers. Students who are out of school because of travel, illness, or other reasons will also be able to get to experience the "lesson" and then can do the discovery work with their class when they return—or better yet, virtually.
Another benefit is the medium of video, which is usually how classes are "flipped" . . . close ups and animations or materials that are not easily worked into lectures can become the main resource for a flipped class. These resources can be accessed at will by the learner, which can be on the football field during a break, on the bus on the way home, or in a library or café. (A. Bellow, personal communication, August 28, 2013)

Shirley Hord, a leader in promoting professional learning communities of teachers, admitted that flipped teaching is new to her. But she was optimistic about its potential:

I see flipped classrooms impacting education if teachers' practices change, to make instruction more relevant and appealing to students, [helping teachers] increasingly address the differentiated needs of all students, plan for and deliver instruction that addresses those needs. . . .

Greatest benefits could be for those students who are mature, disciplined, motivated, and ready to be self-initiating learners . . . those who find the typical classroom boring or less than challenging. The flipped [classroom] reminds me of the college seminar of doctoral level students, where readings are given for out-of-class, and then interaction follows. For students who are critical thinkers, problem solvers, flipped classroom[s] might be a real booster for them . . . and, it goes without saying that teachers will need to learn how to plan for and direct this different structure. (S. Hord, personal communication, September 4, 2013)

WHAT COULD BE THE DOWNSIDES?

As indicated in the *caveats* ending the prior chapters, along with benefits come downsides that need to be addressed. At the forefront of these concerns is ensuring that there is true equity of usage and equal access to the devices and high-speed connections needed for flipping. James Harvey, executive director of the National Superintendents Roundtable, has a perspective on education and change seasoned by his experience as a principal staff writer of, among other works, the 1983 education report *A Nation at Risk* (National Commission on Excellence in Education, 1983).

Harvey noted,

I would expect the greatest benefit would be gained by highly motivated students with easy access to computers in their homes or communities. Would the less motivated be any more likely to do "homework" in a flipped classroom than they are in traditional classrooms? That remains to be seen and might be one of the pedagogical issues requiring attention. Of course without easy access to computers outside the classroom students cannot readily be served by the flipped classroom. Substantial equity considerations need to be taken into account. (J. Harvey, personal communication, September 2, 2013)

Several respondents noted that, without teacher training, flipping could perpetuate the least effective pedagogical practices. Harvey points to other potentially negative impacts on teachers:

> The best teachers already invest 2–3 hours in classroom preparation and evaluation of student work for every hour they spend in the classroom. Developing high quality "lectures" for the flipped classroom is not something that can be done on the fly. It might be the case that flipping a classroom substantially increases teacher workload. (J. Harvey, personal communication, September 2, 2013)

His last caveat is an important one:

> I'd also be concerned that policymakers and "reformers" with little or no experience in schools would be attracted to the idea of a Common Core of scripted lectures (to go along with a lot of scripted curriculum that already exists). If that happened, the vision in your proposal (of individual teachers preparing their own homework) might be pushed aside in favor of a "great lectures" series covering essential parts of the curriculum from Kindergarten through Grade 12. Then we truly would have the "national curriculum" that so many oppose. (J. Harvey, personal communication, September 2, 2013)

WHAT MIGHT PREVENT FLIPPING FROM GAINING TRACTION IN K–12 CLASSROOMS?

A Mismatch Between Content and What Learners Need

Rick Hess, resident scholar and director of education policy at the American Enterprise Institute, and Bror Saxberg, chief learning officer at Kaplan Incorporated, remind us that flipped learning today might lead to an outcome similar to what occurred back when the printing press enabled the brave new world of textbooks:

> The printing press offered the opportunity to do this back in the 15th century—the idea that you could have students read through key concepts and ideas ahead of time, flipping back and forth through content, which should enable a much more engaged conversation with faculty/teachers about practical applications and complex issues not covered by the text.
>
> It didn't work out.
>
> Why not? Because when you look at most textbooks for most students today (or in the past), they were not a good match: students emerged from their "non-class time" still confused by the materials they were exposed to (print, in the past), and hence the teacher had to repeat and reinforce what was supposed to have been learned from the out-of-class materials.
>
> Just because technology and the Internet provide a different form of information that can be absorbed outside of classroom hours does not mean it will be more effective than a textbook. If the media (video, interactives, on-line text, simulations, etc.) is not matched to what students already have mastered in their minds—i.e., are fluent with—there is a good chance that, just as with textbooks, a significant fraction of students will show up in class having been confused by their out-of-class materials (or perhaps not even having engaged with them), leading teachers to confront the same problem they had with textbooks: a significant fraction of students show up without having mastered what they were supposed to before class. (B. Saxberg & R. Hess, personal communication, August 29, 2013)

Imposing This "Solution" on Teachers and Schools

Another barrier to implementation may be pushback and resistance if flipped teaching, like other reform measures in the past, is imposed upon teachers. Greg Green started flipping with just one class at Clintondale High School and carefully built support from the entire staff before declaring the entire building a "flipped high school." He notes,

> You still have to look at things from the perspective of your staff. What's in it for them? How can this help them? They need to be ready to invest extra time when you're making a change of this magnitude. . . . The important thing is to give everyone a chance to innovate without the fear of failure. The bottom line is do you really want to threaten innovation with a stick? (Greg Green as quoted in Pedroza, 2013)

James Harvey agrees:

> I would worry greatly about imposing a "flipped class-rooms" agenda on public schools. I would anticipate that a top-down mandate would generate opposition. It would be much wiser to let this grow organically. As teachers find it useful and helpful, they can become the concept's best sales agents. (J. Harvey, personal communication, September 2, 2013)

The Powerful Backward Pull of Tradition

Innovation is risky and brings with it the threat of failure. Teacher as sage on the stage delivering instruction, worksheets sent home for practice—that's the kind of schooling the public knows best. For some teachers, even using the term "flipping the classroom" is risky. Some find it politically safer to call it "blended instruction" or "blended learning" and talk about how technology is making it possible to do more with class time. Saying "Kids don't do homework anymore" can raise red flags with the public!

And, as one veteran teacher observed,

> The biggest problem with flipped teaching is that, while it is possible to visualize what goes on outside of class—whether that is traditional homework papers or video

lessons—most who are not teaching find it difficult to envision what goes on inside the classroom—flipped or otherwise.

Assessments That Don't Get It

Ed Koch, former Mayor of New York, famously asked his constituents, "How'm I doing?" Teachers and schools are asked this question by a skeptical public on a regular basis. Testing students on local, state, national, or international measures is what typically gives the public their answer.

Tests drive much of what goes on in schools today, but making assessments track the attainment of 21st century skills and knowledge is a huge challenge for the research community. This adoption of Common Core State Standards makes the issue even more important. The U.S. Department of Education invested heavily in the development of tests that will measure how well students meet these standards, but substantial concerns remain. Some states have dropped out of the Common Core movement due to the higher costs of these tests, while others fear public backlash if their students score lower on these new and challenging exams than they have on previous state assessments. It is not surprising that educators are reluctant to adopt new approaches to instruction—including flipped classrooms—in an era of increasing accountability.

Outdated Teacher Accountability Measures

Teacher accountability is as hot a topic in education today as student accountability. Teacher evaluation requirements tied to Race to the Top funding and NCLB waivers, along with huge investments by the Bill and Melinda Gates Foundation and other foundations, have fueled these efforts. Because student test scores are a major factor in teacher accountability measures, teachers have much to lose if their students in this year's class don't do as well as the ones they taught last year. Yet changed curriculum and pedagogical approaches often bring an initial drop in test scores before the educational innovation takes root and the teacher and students are comfortable with it.

Furthermore, most teacher accountability systems are built on the assumption that teaching is done in the traditional mode—the solo teacher working in a closed classroom where that teacher's influence is the sole driver of student learning.

Rick Hess cautions that "many of the teacher evaluation systems calling for "21st century evaluation and pay work only so long as schools cling ever more tightly to the rhythms of Horace Mann's 19th century schoolhouse." As Hess says, the metrics "get real messy" when schools take on other approaches (Hess, 2013).

Some educators who are flipping have been able to shine within these evaluation frameworks. Melissa Wiscount at McKinley High School, profiled in Chapter 1, was proud to report that all of the teachers she taught how to flip their classrooms received 4's (the top rating) on IMPACT, the teacher evaluation system used by the District of Columbia Public Schools (M. Wiscount, personal communication, May 28, 2013). Is this because these innovators were better teachers to start with, or because the kinds of teaching measured on the IMPACT observation sheet are put into practice in flipped classrooms?

This kind of positive feedback has given other teachers in the school confidence to experiment. It also helps that their principal, David Pinder, was supportive of innovation, stating "I want to give them permission to fail." They would not be penalized for trying something new.

Big Money/Big Hype

Flipping has captured the attention of the market. Producers of educational hardware, software, and applications are tailoring products and producing creative new tools that can be used in flipped classrooms. For example, Pearson, the publishing giant, has put its name and money behind the Flipped Learning Network, and has developed a full curriculum of training for the flipped classroom. Other companies are following suit and aggressively reaching out to flipping educators.

Some teachers are worried that commercialization of their homegrown product will dilute the original purity and intent of flipped teaching. They fear the hype for new products and services will raise expectations that teachers may not be able to meet, or aim people in the wrong direction. There is also concern regarding the objectivity and reliability of data and research compiled by those with a financial interest in the product—in this case flipping.

Discussing the "promise and peril" of technology, Diane Ravitch summed up what she called the "conundrum" of technology in schools: Teachers see technology as a tool to inspire student learning; entrepreneurs see it as a way to standardize teaching, to replace teachers, to make money and to market new products. Which vision will prevail? (Ravitch, 2013).

FLIPPED CLASSROOMS: LASTING IMPACT OR PASSING FAD?

Whether flipping will become a mainstay of education is hard to predict. Most of the thought leaders we surveyed agree with James Harvey's position:

I think it's a very promising innovation. It is clear from efforts such as the Khan Academy and MOOCs in higher education that technology enables the delivery of a lot of information directly to many students, on their schedule and at their convenience. It's not a silver bullet but it is more than a fad and could have a significant impact. (J. Harvey, personal communication, September 2, 2013)

Devon Jensen put it this way:

Considering the massive push across Canada, the United States, and Europe to establish 21st Century Learning as the new pedagogical framework for education, I do not see flipped classrooms as merely a fad. Within these new technological pedagogies, there is awareness that both learners and teachers experience the transmission and creation of knowledge in new ways. Beyond this, educators are trying to create global citizens who have control over essential digital literacy skills such as Civic Literacy, Media Literacy, Research Literacy, Cultural Literacy and Economic Literacy. Flipped Classrooms are consistent with 21st Century learning and with the modern ways that students learn, understand, and create thought. In this sense, flipped classrooms are close to the lived experiences of students and will have a major impact on the delivery of educational content. (D. Jensen, personal communication, September 2, 2013)

Once the Genie Is Let Out of the Bottle. . . .

Here's another reason to believe flipping will remain with us:

It is not a new concept to have teachers act as facilitators of learning, but the power that technology affords us to shift some of the pre-learning or pre-investigation to videos or other supplementary pieces of academic content in order to focus on exploration and discovery is remarkable and I feel strongly that we can't put the genie back in the bottle. (A. Bellow, personal communication, August 28, 2013)

Opening the Black Box of Classroom Practice

Longtime observers of school reform cycles point to the persistence of classroom practice that remains little changed from the classrooms of yesterday. Larry Cuban has studied what he calls the "contradiction of enormous structural change in U.S. public schools amid stability in teaching practices" (Cuban, 2013, preface). In what he calls "the black box of classroom practice," Cuban provides an intriguing metaphor for teaching. Unlike the black box recorders that provide evidence of what went wrong when a plane crashes, the black box of classroom practice remains closed, a mystery to those on the outside. Unlike the recorders found in planes, this black box reveals no clues as to why some teachers, and their students, fail to obtain liftoff, reach the desired cruising altitude, or make a successful landing at the end of the trip.

Will flipped classrooms be any different? Advocates would suggest that the transparency offered by flipped lessons may reveal what's in that black box of classroom practice. Watching teachers deliver instruction through flipped teaching videos may lead to discussion of how and what teachers are teaching, midcourse corrections, and better techniques.

Of course, even before flipping, some teachers were video-recording their teaching—for example, preservice teachers, novice teachers, those seeking recognition from the National Board for Professional Teaching Standards—but these videos are typically used for evaluation purposes, not for sharing and reflection. Most teachers had no reason to record their every teaching lesson.

FINAL THOUGHTS: CAN WE FLIP THE FUTURE?

As we come to the end of our top 10 reasons, I return to what first won me over to flipping: seeing great things happening in the classroom when the teachers at Byron High School began to flip their teaching. For me, the real magic came when teachers began to watch each other's lessons as they developed their flipped math curricula. They learned from each other in ways they found intellectually stimulating, personally satisfying, and professionally empowering—the best professional development they'd ever experienced.

In flipping their teaching, these educators are flipping their learning and opening themselves to new ways of thinking. As they and other teachers around the globe share flipped lessons and techniques, they are opening the black box of their classroom practice to new perspectives, approaches, models, and ideas.

How big an impact will this make in education? Is it lasting change? Time will tell. For now, flipping the future lies in the hands of you, the reader. I encourage you to flip your thinking, entertain new ideas, and keep your eyes on opportunities that flipping could provide for making teaching more effective, and learning more lasting, empowering, and engaging. I wish you well in this exciting endeavor!

Appendix

Educators' Q&A on Flipped Classrooms

Q. What's the difference, if any, between "blended learning" and "flipping the classroom"?

A. Blended learning is generally defined as some combination of face-to-face learning and online learning. Flipped teaching falls under the larger umbrella of blended learning, but it is a subset or particular form of blended learning that has its own characteristics.

Q. What are the key characteristics of flipped classrooms?

A. When the classroom is flipped, information that would otherwise be presented during group class time (e.g., a teacher's lecture, video clip, online tutorial, reading, simulation, or demonstration) is made available for the students to access on their individual time as homework. Class time is then used for practice, to build on and apply that information with a variety of hands-on activities (discussion, peer instruction, working on problems, labs, etc.) with the expert (the teacher) there to help the student when questions arise or assistance is needed.

Q. Do I have to make my own video lessons?

A. There are a range of resources, many of which are free, where teachers can access video lessons (see below). But most teachers prefer to make their own lessons, so they can use vocabulary that reflects their curriculum and examples relevant to their students, and maintain the teacher/student bond.

Q. Do I need special equipment to create lessons for the flipped classroom?

A. Teachers can create flipped lessons using hardware they are likely to have in the classroom (i.e., computers, tablets, smartphones, interactive whiteboards, document cameras), and they can download software and applications, many of which are available for free on the Internet. These tools and applications enable them to capture themselves teaching and their lesson materials through screencasts, audiopodcasts, and voicethreads, and then post the lessons online or capture them on a flash drive or CD/DVD. Many commercial products are also available, and more are coming onto the market rapidly to meet the growing demand. For example, an external microphone is highly recommended for recording from a desktop or laptop computer, as clear audio is critical for effective teaching videos.

Q. Where do I store my videos so students have access to them 24/7?

A. Many teachers use YouTube, TeacherTube, or similar online storage sites. Some schools have a learning management system (LMS) where videos can be loaded for students to access. Some school websites allow teachers to upload videos to the teacher's website.

Q. How long should my video lessons be?

A. Teachers advise keeping the videos short, generally dealing with one or two key concepts per video. One guideline suggests approximately one minute for each grade level—that is, 5-minute videos lessons for fifth-grade students, 10-minute lessons for tenth-grade students, etc.

Q. Should I flip my whole course at once?

A. Start small, creating one or two lessons, and build from there. Pay attention to student feedback on the lessons and technique. Even the most ardent flipping teachers don't flip all lessons, every day. However, some recommend flipping at least one full unit, since there will be a learning curve for students (and teachers!) to adjust to the flipped environment.

Q. What if my students do not have access to computers or the Internet at home?

A. Survey students and/or parents prior to flipping to see what technology the family can make available to the student. Lessons can be placed on a flash drive, CD, or DVD if good Internet access is not available. Students can be provided mobile devices to take home (laptops or tablets) or be encouraged to use equipment in school computer labs, libraries, or classrooms before or after class. Personal smartphones are often the technology of choice for students.

Q. How do I know my students have watched the flipped lessons?

A. Teachers often require students to take notes and bring the notes to class or submit them online. Others embed questions that students must answer before moving forward in the video, or at the end to test their knowledge of the material. Some require students to respond to questions like, "What did you learn in this lesson? How does it relate to what you already knew? What questions do you still have?" and submit these before class begins. Some learning management systems allow teachers to track when students watched a video, how many times they watched it, and for how long.

Q. Where can I go for help?

A. There are many sources from which you can get help online. The Flipped Learning Network hosts webinars, podcasts, open houses, and an annual conference. Their website (flippedlearning.org) provides links to resources and blogs, including the NING (http://flippedclassroom .org/, an online platform for a social network), which has over 16,000 members. The Flipped Learning Institute (http://flippedinstitute.org) is another popular website set up as a self-help guide for educators. New sites are popping up rapidly on the web. EdWeb.net, an online community of educators, has a flipped learning community (www .edweb.net/flipped) with resources, discussion groups, and free webinars. There is a Twitter group of educators that meets every Monday evening. Many individual teachers have blog pages that provide guidance, reflections, and links to resources that have worked for them.

Q. How can I find out about good (and free or low-cost) resources for flipping the classroom?

A. Educator blogs are a great way to learn out about free resources, as teachers typically review how well these resources work in their settings. For example, "Educational Technology and Mobile Learning" has descriptions of mobile apps and web tools that can be used for a variety of educational purposes. The section on flipping the classroom (www.educators technology.com/search/label/flipped%20classroom)   is especially comprehensive. Their list of free and simple video tools (www.educatorstechnology.com/2012/06/8-free-and-simple-tools-to-create-video.html) is particularly helpful for guidance on making videos.

Q. What should administrators do to prepare for and support flipped classrooms?

A. Think "TGIF" ("Thank Goodness It's Flipped!"):

Trust your teachers and give them the opportunity to innovate.

Grant them the support they need (time to learn and collaborate, and resources needed).

Inform yourself as school instructional leader/lead learner, and keep the parent community informed of what changes to expect.

Facilitate the changes needed to succeed (e.g., extend the hours of the media center or computer labs; allow students to take school equipment home or use personal devices in the classroom; increase the school wireless network and bandwidth).

References

Anderson, L. W., Krathwohl, D. R., Airasian, P. W., Cruikshank, K. A., Mayer, R. E., Pintrich, P. R., . . . Wittrock, M. C. (2000). *A taxonomy for learning, teaching, and assessing: A revision of Bloom's taxonomy of educational objectives.* New York, NY: Pearson, Allyn & Bacon.

Assessment and Teaching of 21st Century Skills (ATC21S). (n.d.). *What are 21st Century Skills?* Retrieved January 22, 2014, from http://atc21s.org/index.php/about/what-are-21st-century-skills/

Bergmann, J., & Sams, A. (2012). *Flip your classroom: Reach every student in every class every day.* Eugene, OR: International Society for Technology in Education.

Bergmann, J., & Sams, A. (2013a, April 30). *Flipped learning primer part II: Flipped-mastery learning.* Retrieved from http://home.edweb.net/flipped-learning-primer-part-ii-flipped-mastery-learning/

Bergmann, J., & Sams, A. (2013b, June 17). *Keynote address.* FlipCon 13, Stillwater, MN.

Bloom B. S. (1956). *Taxonomy of educational objectives, handbook I: The cognitive domain.* New York, NY: David McKay.

Bloom, B. S. (1981). *All our children learning.* New York, NY: McGraw-Hill.

Bodie, G. D., Powers, W. G., & Fitch-Hauser, M. (2006). Chunking, priming and active learning: Toward an innovative and blended approach to teaching communications-related skills. *Interactive Learning Environments, 14*(2), 119–135. Retrieved from http://www.psych.ufl.edu/~abrams/cognition/Articles/bodie_et_al_06.pdf

Bransford, J. D., Brown, A. L., & Cocking, R. (Eds.). (1999). *How people learn: Brain, mind, experience, and school.* Washington, DC: National Academy Press.

Bruner, J. (1960). *The process of education.* Cambridge, MA: Harvard University Press.

Bruner, J. (1966). *Toward a theory of instruction.* Cambridge, MA: Harvard University Press.

Bui, L. (2013, August 26). At schools, the word of the day is 'new.' *The Washington Post,* Metro section, pp. 1–2.

Burton, A. (2012, July 12). *Bienvenue à la classe de français!* Parent survey. Retrieved from http://www.mrsburton.com/?p=958

Burton, A. (2013, August 28). Cooperative learning for the workplace [Web log post]. Retrieved from http://mmeburton.blogspot.com

Carroll, T. G., Fulton, K., & Doerr, H. (2010). *Team up for 21st century teaching and learning. What research and practice reveal about professional learning.* Washington, DC: National Commission on Teaching and America's Future.

Center for Applied Special Technology (CAST). (2011) *Universal design for learning guidelines version 2.0.* Wakefield MA: Author. Retrieved from http://www.udlcenter.org/sites/udlcenter .org/files/updateguidelines2_0.pdf

Christensen, C. (2013). *Disruptive innovation.* Retrieved from http:// www.claytonchristensen.com/key-concepts

Clark, D. (2007, December 19) 10 reasons to dump lectures [Web log post]. Retrieved from http://donaldclarkplanb.blogspot .ca/2007/12/10-reasons-to-dump-lectures.html

Clark, R., & Mayer, R. (2011). *E-learning and the science of instruction* (3rd ed.) San Francisco, CA: John Wiley & Sons.

Crouch, C. H., & Mazur, E. (2001). Peer instruction: Ten years of experience and results. *American Journal of Physics, 69*(9), 970–977.

Crouch, C. H., Watkins, J., Fagen, A. P., & Mazur, E. (2007). Peer instruction: Engaging students one-on-one, all at once. In *Research-Based Reform of University Physics, Vol. 1*(1), 40–95. Retrieved from http://mazur.harvard.edu/sentFiles/Mazur_278963.pdf

Cuban, L. (2013). *Inside the black box of classroom practice: Change without reform in American education.* Cambridge, MA: Harvard Education Press.

Darling-Hammond, L., Chung Wei, R., Andree, A., Richardson, N., & Orphanos, S. (2009). *Professional learning in the learning profession: A status report on teacher development in the United States and abroad.* Washington, DC: National Staff Development Council.

Dede, C. (2010). Comparing frameworks for 21st century skills. In J. Bellanca & R. Brandt (Eds.), *21st Century Skills* (pp. 51–76). Bloomington, IN: Solution Tree Press.

Dewey, J. (2001 [1915]). *The school and society and the child and the curriculum.* Mineola, NY: Courier Dover.

Evans, J. (2014, January 30). *Ten things everyone should know about students and digital learning: Speak Up 2013 national findings.* Presentation at FETC annual conference, Orlando, FL. Retrieved from http://www.tomorrow.org/speakup/TenThings_DigitalLearning_pres.html

Faulkner, T., & Warneke, R. (2013, June 19). *So you flipped your classroom. Now what?* Presentation at Flip Con 13, Stillwater, MN. Retrieved from https://sites.google.com/a/byron.k12.mn.us/byron-high-school-mathematics-department

Federal Communications Commission. (2013, July 23). Notice of proposed rulemaking, Paragraph 2. Retrieved from http://transition.fcc.gov/Daily_Releases/Daily_Business/2013/db0723/FCC-13-100A1.pdf

Fletcher, G., Schaffhauser, D., & Levin, D. (2012). *Out of print: Reimagining the K–12 textbook in a digital age.* Washington, DC: State Educational Technology Directors Association (SETDA). Retrieved from http://www.setda.org/c/document_library/get_file?folderId=321&name=DLFE-1598.pdf

Flip. (n.d.). *Macmillan dictionary.* Retrieved February 8, 2013, from http://www.macmillandictionary.com/us/dictionary/american/flip

Flip. (1939). *Webster's collegiate dictionary* (5th ed.). Springfield, MA: G. & C. Merriam.

Flipped Learning Panel. (2013, June 18). Panel of parents and students at FlipCon13, Stillwater, MN.

Fulton, K., & Britton, T. (2011). *STEM teachers in professional learning communities: From good teachers to great teaching.* Washington, DC: National Commission on Teaching and America's Future.

Fung, B. (2014, February 4). Here's Obama's plan to give teachers and libraries $1 billion a year in extra funding. *The Washington Post* (online). Retrieved from http://www.washingtonpost.com/blogs/the-switch/wp/2014/02/04/heres-obamas-plan-to-give-teachers-and-libraries-1-billion-a-year-in-extra-funding//?print=1

Goutell, S., Heimbigner, N., Maybee, A., Maxey, J., McCandless, T., & Tierney, S. (2012, May 23). *Differentiating through the flipping process. Pre-Approval: Application for LPS Credit-Action Research,* Littleton Public Schools, CO.

Green, J., & Fulton, K. (2013, July 17). *Top ten reasons to flip the classroom.* Presentation to Southern Regional Education Board meeting, Charlotte, NC.

Halla, K. (2013, August 29). How to start your students on the flipped experience [Web log post]. Retrieved from http://worldhistoryeducatorsblog.blogspot.com

Hamdan, N., McKnight, P., McKnight, K., & Arfstrom, K. M. (2013). *A review of flipped learning.* Flipped Learning Network. Retrieved from http://www.flippedlearning.org/cms/lib07/VA01923112/Centricity/Domain/41/LitReview_FlippedLearning.pdf

Hess, F. M., & Saxberg, B. (2013). *Breakthrough leadership in the digital age: Using learning science to reboot schooling.* Thousand Oaks, CA: Corwin.

Hess, R. (2013, September 11). Teacher Quality 2.0 [Web log post]. Retrieved from http://blogs.edweek.org/edweek/rick_hess_straight_up/2013/09/teacher_quality_20.html

Johnson, G. (2012, May 14). *The flipped classroom as a vehicle to the future* [Video]. Retrieved from http://www.youtube.com/watch?v=ZpHfTO8SW7U

Johnson, G. (2013). *Student perceptions of the flipped classroom* (Master's thesis, College of Graduate Studies, University of British Columbia, Kelowna). Available at https://circle.ubc.ca/handle/2429/44070

Johnson, L. W., & Renner, J. D. (2012). *Effect of the flipped classroom model on a secondary computer applications course: Student and teacher perceptions, questions and student achievement* (Doctoral dissertation, College of Education and Human Development, University of Louisville, Kentucky). Retrieved from http://theflippedclassroom.files.wordpress.com/2012/04/johnson-renner-2012.pdf

Joseph, C. (Aug. 1, 2012). *Introduction to Ms. Joseph flip math classroom* [Video]. Retrieved from http://www.youtube.com/watch?v=t5SKcolyh-E

Khan Academy. (n.d.) *60 minutes: The future of education?* [Video]. Retrieved September 30, 2013, from https://www.khanacademy.org/talks-and-interviews/key-media-pieces/v/khan-academy--the-future-of-education

Kharbach, M. (n.d.) *25 Important skills for 21st century students.* Retrieved February 8, 2104, from http://www.educatorstechnology.com/2013/11/25-important-skills-for-21st-century.html

Lage, M. J., Platt, G. J., & Treglia, M. (2000). Inverting the classroom: A gateway to creating an inclusive learning environment. *Journal of Economic Education*, *31*(1) 30–43. Retrieved from http://dl .dropbox.com/u/249331/Inverted_Classroom_Paper.pdf

Lanier, K. (2013, June 18). *Demystify flip for parents*. Presentation at FlipCon13, Stillwater, MN.

Levin, D. A. (2011). Digital content: Making learning relevant. *Principal Leadership*, *12*(1), 32–36. Retrieved from http://www .setda.org/c/document_library/get_file?folderId=300&name= DLFE-1356.pdf

Mazur, E. (1991, January/February). Can we teach computers to teach? *Computers in Physics*, *5*, 31–38. Retrieved from http:// mazur.harvard.edu/sentFiles/Mazur_256459.pdf

Mazur, E. (2009, November 12). *Confessions of a converted lecturer* [Video]. Retrieved from http://www.youtube.com/ watch?v=WwslBPj8GgI

Mendel, H. (2012, June 18). *Students' flipped classroom @ OKM* [Video]. Retrieved from http://www.youtube.com/ watch?v=dLcO6zZd0yw

MetLife. (2009). *The MetLife survey of the American teacher: Collaborating for student success*. New York, NY: Metropolitan Life Insurance Company.

Microsoft Partners in Learning, The Pearson Foundation, & Gallup. (2013, May 28). *21st Century skills and the workplace*. Retrieved from http://www.gallup.com/strategicconsulting/162821/21st-century-skills-workplace.aspx

Miller, G. A. (1956). The magical number seven, plus or minus two: Some limits on our capacity for processing information. *The Psychological Review*, *63*(2), 81–97.

Morris, C., & Thomasson, A. (n.d.a). *Frequently asked questions*. Retrieved September 30, 2013, from http://www.flippedlearningjournal .org/faq.html

Morris, C., & Thomasson, A. (n.d.b). *Thomasson Morris instruction*. Retrieved September 30, 2013, from http://www.flipped learningjournal.org/cheryl-and-andrew.html

Morris, C., Thomasson, A., Lindgren-Streicher, K., Kirch, C., & Baker, K. (2012, July 28). *Thomasson and Morris flip the English classroom: So you want to flip your class*. Retrieved from http:// www.morrisflipsenglish.com/1/post/2012/07/so-you-want-to-flip-your-class.html

Mull, B. (2011, December 19). Learn from a school that has completely flipped out: An interview with Greg Green on flipped learning model. *November learning.* Retrieved from http://novemberlearning.com/an-interview-with-greg-green-on-flipped-learning-model/

Musallam, R. (n.d.). Speakers. Ramsey Musallam: Educator on TED ideas worth spreading. Retrieved from http://www.ted.com/speakers/ramsey_musallam.html

Musallam, R. (2013a, April). *3 rules to spark learning* [Video]. TED talk for education. Retrieved from http://www.ted.com/talks/ramsey_musallam_3_rules_to_spark_learning.html

Musallam, R. (2013b, January 5). *A pedagogy-first approach to the flipped classroom.* Retrieved September 30, 2013, from http://www.cyclesoflearning.com/9/category/Commentary/1.html

Musallam, R. (2013c, June 19). *Explore-flip-apply: Using video to empower the learning cycle.* Keynote presentation, FlipCon13, Stillwater, MN.

National Center of Education Statistics (NCES). (n.d.). *Fast facts.* Retrieved September 30, 2013, from http://nces.ed.gov/fastfacts/display.asp?id=46

National Commission on Excellence in Education. (1983). *A nation at risk.* Washington, DC: U.S. Department of Education.

O'Mahony, T. K., Vye, N. J., Bransford, J. D., Sanders, E. A., Stevens, R., Stephens, R. D., . . . Soleiman, M. K. (2012). A comparison of lecture-based and challenge-based learning in a workplace setting: Course designs, patterns of interactivity, and learning outcomes. *Journal of the Learning Sciences, 21,* 182–206. doi: 10.1080/10508406.2011.611775

Partnership for 21st Century Skills. (n.d.) *Framework for 21st century living: An overview.* Retrieved January 22, 2014, from http://www.p21.org/about-us/p21-framework

Pearson Education. (2013). *Flipped learning model dramatically improves course pass rate for at-risk students. Clintondale High School.* Pearson case study. Retrieved September 30, 2013, from http://assets.pearsonschool.com/asset_mgr/current/201317/Clintondale_casestudy.pdf

Pedagogy. (1993). *Webster's third new international dictionary of the English language, unabridged.* Springfield, MA: Webster.

Pedroza, A. (2013, May 13). Don't threaten innovation with a stick: Principal Greg Green spells out what leaders need to flip [Web log post]. Retrieved from http://flippedinstitute.org/blog/?p=508

Piaget, J. (1964). Part I: Cognitive development in children: Piaget development and learning. *Journal of Research in Science Teaching,* 2(3): 176–186. doi: 10.102/tea.3660020306

Project Tomorrow. (2012a, May). *Personalizing the classroom experience: Teachers, librarians and administrators connect the dots with digital learning.* Speak Up 2011 national findings K–12 Educators. Retrieved from http://www.tomorrow.org/speakup/SU11_PersonalizedClassroom_EducatorsReport.html#sthash.bZ6mRVBD.dpuf

Project Tomorrow (2012b). *Digital learning in 2012: Challenges and opportunities for school and district administrators.* Retrieved from http://www.tomorrow.org/speakup/pdfs/Infographic_DigitalLearning2012_Educators.pdf

Project Tomorrow. (2013a). *Do you know? Ten things everyone should know about K–12 students' views on digital learning.* Speak Up 2012 national research project findings. Retrieved from http://www.tomorrow.org/speakup/pdfs/SU2012_StudentTop10.pdf

Project Tomorrow. (2013b). *From chalkboards to tablets: The digital conversion of the K–12 classroom.* Speak Up 2012 national findings educators and parent. Retrieved from http://www.tomorrow.org/speakup/SU12_DigitalConversion_EducatorsReport.html

Project Tomorrow. (2013c). *From chalkboards to tablets: The emergence of the K–12 digital learner.* Speak Up 2012 national findings K–12 students. Retrieved from http://www.tomorrow.org/speakup/SU12_DigitalLearners_StudentReport.html

Project Tomorrow and Flipped Learning Network. (2014). *Speak Up 2013 national research project findings: A second year review of flipped learning.* Retrieved from http://www.tomorrow.org/speakup/pdfs/SU13SurveyResultsFlippedLearning.pdf

Public Broadcasting System (PBS). (2013, February 4). *PBS survey finds teachers are embracing digital resources to propel student learning* [Press release]. Retrieved from http://www.pbs.org/about/news/archive/2013/teacher-tech-survey

Purcell, K., Buchanan, J., & Friedrich, L. (2013, July 16). *The impact of digital tools on student writing and how writing is taught in schools.* Pew Research Center's Internet and American Life Project. Retrieved from http://pewinternet.org/Reports/2013/Teachers-technology-and-writing

Ravitch, D. (2013, August 1). Three dubious uses of technology in education [Web log post]. Retrieved from http://dianeravitch.net/2013/08/01/three-dubious-uses-of-technology-in-education/

Reich, J. (2013, June 14). Shockingly similar digital divide findings from 1998 and 2013 [Web blog post]. Retrieved from http://blogs .edweek.org/edweek/edtechresearcher/2013/06/shockingly_similar_digital_divide_findings_from_1998_and_2013.html

Reynolds, R. (2012, February 12). *E-textbook market remains on course to pass 25% by 2015.* Next is now. Retrieved from http://www .nextisnow.net/blog/e-textbook-market-remains-on-course-to-pass-25-by-2015.html

Ruhl, K. L., Hughes, C. A., & Schloss, P. J. (1987). Using the pause procedure to enhance lecture recall. *Teacher Education and Special Education, 10*(1), 14–18.

Sams, A. (2013, June 18). *Keynote address.* FlipCon 2013, Stillwater, MN.

Schaffhauser, D. (2014, March 27). Report: Most schools delivering BYOD programs, traning teachers in mobile devices usage. *The Journal.* Retrieved from http://thejournal.com/articles/2014/03/27/report-most-schools-delivering-byod-programs-training-teachers-in-mobile-devices-usage.aspx

Schrock, K. (2013). *Bloomin' apps.* Kathy Schrock's guide to everything. Retrieved from http://www.schrockguide.net/bloomin-apps.html

Tononi, G., & Cirelli, C. (2013) Perchance to prune. *Scientific American, 309*(2), 34–39.

U.S. Congress, Office of Technology Assessment. (1988). *Power on! New tools for teaching and learning.* OTA-SET-379. Washington, DC: U.S. Government Printing Office.

Vygotsky, L. S. (1978). *Mind in society: Development of higher psychological processes.* Cambridge, MA: Harvard University Press.

Wilson, H. (2013a, October 25). Introducing alternative assessment & peer instruction in the flipped class: Week 7 reflections [Web log post]. Retrieved from http://wilsonsflippedlab.blogspot.com

Wilson, H. (2013b, September 14). Reflections on my first attempt at flipped learning [Web log post]. Retrieved from http://wilsonsflippedlab.blogspot.com

Index

CORWIN

A SAGE Company

The Corwin logo—a raven striding across an open book—represents the union of courage and learning. Corwin is committed to improving education for all learners by publishing books and other professional development resources for those serving the field of PreK–12 education. By providing practical, hands-on materials, Corwin continues to carry out the promise of its motto: **"Helping Educators Do Their Work Better."**